# VETERANS ADMINISTRATION CLAIMS

# VETERANS ADMINISTRATION CLAIMS

## WHAT YOU NEED TO KNOW TO BE SUCCESSFUL

### BY THE POPULAR VA BLOGGER
# ASKNOD

Copyright © 2012 by Asknod.

Library of Congress Control Number: 2012912208
ISBN: Hardcover 978-1-4771-3951-6
Softcover 978-1-4771-3950-9
Ebook 978-1-4771-3952-3

All rights reserved. No part of this book may be reproduced or transmitted in any form or by any means, electronic or mechanical, including photocopying, recording, or by any information storage and retrieval system, without permission in writing from the copyright owner.

This book was printed in the United States of America.

**To order additional copies of this book, contact:**
Xlibris Corporation
1-888-795-4274
www.Xlibris.com
Orders@Xlibris.com
116312

# Dedication

This book is dedicated to the memory of Charles Edwin Engle, born February 8, 1945 and died February 22, 1971, Captain (promoted posthumously) of the United States Air Force Reserve. He is the sole reason I'm not room temperature and still on this side of the grass.

# TABLE OF CONTENTS

| | | |
|---|---|---|
| Foreword | | ix |
| Chapter 1 | | 1 |
| | A. My Military Experiences | 1 |
| | B. After the War | 5 |
| | C. History of VA Claims Process | 23 |
| Chapter 2 | Beginning the Process | 29 |
| | A. VSO Representatives | 29 |
| | B. Going at It Alone Pro Se | 31 |
| | C. Getting Your Records | 35 |
| | D. What Records? | 36 |
| Chapter 3 | The Recipe—Filing a Claim | 39 |
| | A. Dos and Don'ts | 39 |
| | B. Beginning the Claim—Basics | 46 |
| | C. Collecting the Evidence | 54 |
| | D. Organizing the Evidence | 55 |
| | E. The Meat of the Claim—Your Nexus Letter(s) | 59 |
| | F. Overwhelming Evidence in SMRs that Precludes Need for Nexus | 66 |
| | G. Proceed to Go! Push Print | 67 |

| Chapter 4 | The Denial | 73 |
|---|---|---|
| | A. The First Denial at the RO | 73 |
| | B. New and Material Evidence Submittal | 82 |
| | C. Appeals Time Limits Filing the Notice of Disagreement (NOD) | 83 |
| | D. DRO Hearing and Review? | 84 |
| | E. SOC and SSOC Time Limits | 87 |
| | F. Form 9s | 89 |
| | G. Hearing or No Hearing? | 92 |
| | H. BVA Waiver of VARO Review | 93 |
| | I. BVA Motions for Reconsideration | 95 |
| | J. CAVC: The Court of Appeals for Veterans Claims | 95 |
| | K. About the Court and How It Works | 98 |
| Chapter 5 | You Win (Or Did You?) | 103 |
| | A. What's Next? | 103 |
| | B. Fenderson or Staged Ratings | 113 |
| | C. You Win in DC | 114 |
| | D. Attaining 100 Percent Schedular Ratings | 115 |
| | E. Total Disability Due To Individual Unemployment or TDIU | 118 |
| | F. Going for Permanent and Total | 119 |
| Chapter 6 | Clear and Unmistakable Error (Cue) Filings | 123 |
| Chapter 7 | Earlier Effective Date via 38 CFR §3.156(c) | 125 |
| Chapter 8 | 38 CFR §3.156(b) | 129 |
| Chapter 9 | VR&E Filings for the Independent Living Program | 131 |
| Chapter 10 | Example of an Initial Claim Using HCV as an Example | 135 |

# FOREWORD

This book is written for the 8 percent of you who have served in the military. That's approximately 26 million as of 2012. Many of you were injured and never sought compensation for it. No one told me to walk off base in 1973 and file with the VA, nor did they tell me I could. I'm sure it wasn't a big secret, but it certainly wasn't advertised. Now we are older, and some of those injuries are starting to become apparent. VA has many ploys to *prevent* you from receiving compensation for this. You may apply for a pension if you are totally disabled by non-service-connected injuries, but this is no reward. It's an either/or proposition—VA pension or SSI/SSD. VA, in most cases, won't grant a pension until you attain the age of sixty-five. The only thing that can be said for a pension is that if you are 100 percent disabled, it generally pays more than SSI. However, if you are entitled to VA compensation, it is tax-free. You can also collect the SSD/SSI in addition to the VA compensation. This is the major distinction between the two types of VA funds.

There is one thing you should know about the Veterans of the Vietnam era. We are dying at an exponentially higher rate than other classes of Vets (i.e., Korea or WW2). Sixty-six percent have already passed away, and the war ended only thirty seven years ago. I attribute that to the wealth of injuries we temporarily survived over all this time and some of the unique diseases caused by Agent Orange. Hepatitis C is a huge component of this too.

You are going to discover many things when you enter the VA claims system. You will be seeking compensation for your injuries/diseases. A denial is almost a given the first time out. This separates the ribbon clerks from the poker players. Ribbon clerks were the mousy Western Union fellows at the train depot in the TV series *Gunsmoke*. You get the idea. If you are not prepared for a long battle, this is a waste of time. We are talking as many as eight to ten years in some cases. If the evidence is clear-cut, it can still be several years. The idea is to wait you out and cause you to lose interest. Decades of evidence suggests their technique is very successful.

Do the arithmetic. Somewhere in excess of 1.2 million claims are filed at regional offices annually. Only fifty thousand a year are appealed to the BVA, and 22 percent win. Only five thousand a year are appealed to the CAVC, and 70 percent of the five thousand see another day and usually a win. You won't get those odds in Las Vegas. You may spend some money on postage, but the amount will come back a thousandfold. Vets are not given to complaining much, and many lose heart when they are denied. VSOs do not talk about these figures. They are in the volume business. Everybody's a winner in their book. Jeez, they even have the compensation rate tables out there handy to look at when you arrive showing the untold riches that await you. Not one of them ever told me about the need for a nexus letter though.

The VA almost forces you to do this with the help of a Veterans Service organization (VSO). If you know what you're doing, you can try this yourself. You are not entitled to the services of an attorney unless and until you lose the initial claim. You can see why this wet blanket approach makes many give up. Veterans are accustomed to getting short shrift from the VA. Besides, who ever heard of a legal process that precludes the use of attorneys at the outset?

This book will show you many things you can do to avoid the mistakes most make. It will show you how to do it yourself rather than depend on the VSO path. The ugly truth is VSOs are nothing more than glorified mailmen. They have no attorney credentials and little or no training in this field. Many are not even Veterans. They receive a salary from the government for representing you and filing your paperwork. They are located inside regional offices and have access to your file. This gives them little more than the ability to tell you why it's taking so long. You can accomplish everything they do and win without the annoyance of someone between you and the agency you are filing your claim with. In fact, chances are your evidence will be filed more successfully if *you* do it. Every time you introduce a new cog in the machine, something can happen. We won't go into Murphy's Law, but the comparison is obvious.

VSOs may say that they have the ability to discuss your claim directly with the rater and do some bartering. That is what you don't want. If you have hearing loss, you do not want to settle for tinnitus at 10 percent. You want that plus hearing loss for 40 percent. When you let someone else speak for you and not even consult you, you will end up being screwed. Don't read about it afterwards.

The difference between most self-help DIY VA claims and this book is simple. After twenty-three years of dealing with this insurance company, I have observed all the things VA does to impede your success. Misrepresentation of evidence, misinterpretation of same, and a bad habit of denying you are what they do. They do not face a demotion or a bad progress report from their supervisors if their efforts have a 60 percent error rate. This would get you fired anywhere else. They are the only game in town, and they know it. Instead of a simpleminded book that says "Insert claim here and wait," my method is dynamic and based on skirting their defenses. If you know ahead of time what it is they are going to use to deny you with, you simply cover *all* the bases. When this happens, they just grant your claim. It's like a vertical slope with no cracks to get a grip on. They rarely encounter this and don't cover the possibility in their manuals.

Veterans who file for themselves have better success if they know what they're doing. This book will not guarantee you a win, but it will show you how not to lose. Every claim is unique, and having the evidence is the reason you will succeed. There is also a lot of proof that the longer you fight them, the greater the chance of a win. This is the squeaky wheel theory. VA tires of fighting a claim for years and will sometimes give in to get rid of you if it has merit. It also appears that in more than 60 percent of cases, the VA is pretty much unjustified in denying you. This is usually discovered on appeal and is the reason I said you might spend a decade on it.

Veterans aren't prepared to win a claim because they assume the VA is there *for* them. Wrong. VA is there to defend the gates against you. The Veterans Administration rightfully should be named the Anti-Veterans Administration. I know that sounds dumb. They have limited financial assets ($126.9 billion) and are stingy about handing them out. Like any government entity, they guard their domain jealously. You are going to attempt to breach this defense. Be prepared for some rude surprises. You will encounter them but will be pleasantly surprised that you prepared ahead of time. VA speaks of a Veteran-friendly environment in which to make our claims. The informal ex parte system of justice is often cited. If it is so Veteran friendly, then why are you forbidden to have an attorney and they can employ five hundred against you?

You will see the word "Veteran" and "Vet" capitalized throughout this book. This is not a misprint. Veterans are those who served in the military; veterans (uncapitalized) are those who have been around a while on the job or who have more job experience. With all due respect to first responders, they are veterans as they serve a local interest, not a national one.

Now, Young Skywalker, wipe that defecation-eating smile off your face. VA is going to get down and dirty with you. They will put on the smiley mask and repeat that famous "We are here to make sure you get what's coming to you" phrase, which means so much more. They will pretend they're bending over backward to understand what it is you want. They will claim they collected all the evidence when they haven't. They lose things regularly because it's a paper system. At the end, statistics tell us you are going to get the Dear John letter. That will be the 85 percent scenario if you *don't* read this book.

```
      \\!//
      (o o)
 -oOOo-(_)-oOOo-
```

# CHAPTER 1

*NOD, Dad, and Uncle Jay (WW2 POW)*

## A
## My Military Experiences

I was a military brat. My father was a fighter pilot in the Air Force and retired after thirty-three years. I enlisted on October 1, 1969 in Virginia in the Air Force. With a draft number of 39, I was due to be drafted in a month. The Army didn't thrill me. I had good test scores in electronics and went into that field. After graduating from telephone installation and maintenance, I had visions of going to England or Italy. Spain was my third choice. I got Thailand to begin with. I arrived on May 15, 1970.

Because I spoke French, I was asked to volunteer for an interpreter job in Cambodia with forward air control pilots. This was the highly classified RUSTIC program that originated when we invaded Cambodia in May 1970. It was run directly from the White House. The assignment changed to Laos a week before my deployment in late July 1970. I was wounded there in September 1970 and returned to Thailand. I got another assignment to NW Thailand to a small forward operating location in October 1970. In December, I noticed I was fatigued and was losing weight. I happened to look in the mirror right after New Year's and noticed that my eyes seemed a little yellow. On the eleventh of January 1971, I entered the local civilian hospital for hepatitis. There was no testing then to determine which type you had. If it went away in short order, it was infectious hepatitis A. If it lingered for weeks, then it was assumed to be the viral type, or hepatitis B. Doctors didn't have alphabetic designations then. The hepatitis diagnosis came eighty-nine days after my wound and transfusion. No one related it to that. After six weeks as an inpatient, I was released to six weeks' light duty and my next misadventures.

I was injured several times within a two-month period later in 1971. It started with an airplane crash in April while laying cable from the air. The pilot pulled up too quickly and stalled the aircraft at low altitude. Fortunately, we walked away from it. I was standing in the back paying the cable out the cargo door when we augered in.

Simultaneously, we were suffering extensive sabotage to our cables on telephone poles off base. After the aircraft accident, I had started to recover from the back pain. We repaired a section of cable, at about 3:00 a.m. one morning in June 1971 that had been damaged. Later, during daylight, we went back and made permanent repairs. A Captain was being very helpful by pulling the new cable up tight with his jeep and a rope. He pulled on it one last time, and the cable went higher than my ladder leaning against it. I bailed off the ladder at the last moment to avoid it and landed right on my ass the same way I did in the aircraft accident. This left me in pain for weeks. I limped around and finally went to the local hospital. They injected my lower back with cortisone and resolved the pain for a time. When it became unbearable, I'd go back in and receive another shot. It was very difficult to communicate with the Thai medical personnel as they spoke no English, and my Thai was pretty limited.

There were no military medical facilities within four hundred kilometers. We received our care from the civilian hospital (McCormick) contracted by the U.S. government. The hospital was used by all the military personnel assigned there as well as the U.S. consulate staff and the Air America/USAID/USIA guys. This was the beginning of my problem. When I left in 1972, those records were never put in my military medical records. It's obvious that there is a gap from September 1970 to July 1972 because there are no entries from military hospitals. A single entry in 1971 stated I was approved for remote/isolated assignments, but that was an assessment required annually and did not require my presence at a military medical facility.

I came home in May of 1972 and went on leave. I reported for duty in California on June 15, 1972. As soon as I was settled in, I promptly reported to the base hospital to find out what was wrong. They found nothing and implied I was malingering. I reported several more times to sick call and finally was scheduled for a full orthopedic workup in March 1973. I was discharged on February 21, and the evaluation was never done.

I was discharged for "antisocial personality with passive aggressive tendencies." I received a general discharge under honorable conditions. This was eight years before they invented PTSD in 1981. For two years in Southeast Asia, the major concern was how well I spoke French and how well I performed my duties. When I came back, it devolved into how well I saluted and how shiny my boots were. Haircuts were more important than what you could hit at 160 yards with an M16. The whole dynamic of war changed back into one of rigid adherence to rules and regulations. I simply couldn't adapt and was booted after three years and four months of faithful service. They said I had "gone native."

# B
# After the War

After watching me suffer in silence for almost a decade, my wife insisted I seek compensation for my back problems. She had already pushed me into medical care for it much earlier in 1984. The back pain was occasional and unpredictable. The only guaranteed thing about it was that it returned fairly regularly and seemed to follow physical exertion.

I almost began the claims process in 1975, but I got a new job and could not afford to take the time off. Work was hard to find then. The Arab oil embargo had resulted in the even/odd day gas lines. I let it go until I couldn't stand it anymore.

I applied for benefits in Seattle at their regional office and used the Disabled American Veterans (DAV). My representative, Ronald Ampe, was very pleasant but not the easiest person to reach. DAV filed my claim July 1989, and I was scheduled shortly thereafter for my Compensation and Pension (C&P) exam to find out the severity of my injuries. The exam on September 25, 1989, was very brief and only involved my hearing issues. I tried to point out that I had multiple issues requiring investigation but was ignored. Ron was unavailable, so I didn't get a back examination. What I wasn't prepared for was the sight that greeted me at the VA Medical Center. There were several Veterans in wheelchairs just outside the front door, smoking and enjoying the fall weather. They were both double amputees and my age. I almost turned around and left. It was hard to think about my problems as being in the same league. VA had recently outlawed smoking indoors. Now they were forced outside. They were a real deterrent to me and my little problems. I have since gotten over the guilt of that day. The more ill I become now, the angrier I get. I want all of you to understand that the government made a bargain with you at enlistment to take care of you for your injuries that happened in service. You are simply making a claim on that promise. You shouldn't have to beg them to honor this commitment.

I was denied for all the claims in January 1990 and began what many of you will run into if you do this. I filed for reconsideration based on no back exam and requested a decision review officer hearing at the regional office

(RO) to explain my case. This was granted, and a hearing was scheduled for July 1990. I wanted a sit down with Mr. Ampe before, but he was unavailable until the day of the hearing. I arrived early and went over what I hoped to accomplish with him. This was when I first got the feeling that his legal help was going to be of little or no use. He didn't remember me, and he certainly didn't remember my case. He tried cramming for it by reading for ten minutes straight before we were invited in.

When I filed, I thought the VA was set up specifically for us and was on our side. My denial felt like an accident at first. Many thoughts rushed through my mind. VA simply didn't have all the info. Someone screwed up. Once the facts were known, this would all be cleared up. The DAV was a large organization, and they had so many to help. Ron's availability was limited by the number of Vets he was helping. The thought that this was going to be an adversarial process never entered my mind. When I look back, I am shocked at how stupid I was. I ignored all the warning signs because the *Veterans Administration* was my defender and protector.

We presented my claim in the best light, but one thing became apparent. The records from McCormick Hospital in Thailand were nowhere to be seen. I told them where to find them. I explained that these records would document the injury and later treatment prior to my return to the United States. I even explained what was in them. VA made absolutely no effort to retrieve them. I was subsequently denied a second time in the decision review of October 1990 and filed my Form 9.

At that time, I also submitted a small portion of the records from Thailand that I had received after calling and asking for them. VA looked at them, or said they did, but continued the denial. The case proceeded to DC and the BVA. By now I was beginning to see a pattern that worried me. VA was an agency of the government. They don't care how long it takes. They don't work as fast as we do. Change was in the works, but it wasn't going to benefit Veterans like me. The war in Southwest Asia was ramping up, and the VA was beginning to see a new wave of applicants. Ron told me I would get the justice I sought at the BVA. They would see the mistake. They were real lawyers there in DC. He lied. What he didn't say was their Disabled American Veterans representative in D. C. was no more a lawyer than he was. The term collusion is too strong, but this does smack of good old boy networking between the VSOs and the VA. That is my personal opinion.

I was denied in March 1992, over my objections that the record was incomplete. Mr. Ampe was excited that we had won on the tinnitus issue. He told me not to pursue the appeal any higher on the back issue because there was no evidence to support it. This was the beginning of the Court of Veterans Appeals (COVA). I believed him. I took his advice and later received a 0 percent rating for my ears and the tinnitus. Again, he thought this was great news and pointed out how I would now be eligible for free hearing aids. For what? To amplify the ringing in my ears? That was the end of my dealings with the DAV, and I was prepared to put paid to the VA as well. "For he who shall have borne the battle" was beginning to ring hollow. My VA score now was an ice cream cone with two scoops of air.

As this was winding down, my wife also was concerned that my skin, especially the upper side of my hands and forearms, was becoming lacerated by mechanical trauma from normal wear and tear. Simply banging my hand against a board caused major damage. I went to my doctors for a year or more, trying to find the cause. They diagnosed it as subcutaneous staph or strep infections and hosed me with antibiotics. It didn't help. I finally went to a dermatologist in November 1992 who identified it straight away as Porphyria Cutanea Tarda (PCT). He surmised it was a secondary from either the hepatitis I had in service in 1971 or my exposure to Agent Orange. This prompted a whole new investigation into my liver. We had seen a newscast about Agent Orange on TV in late 1991, and PCT had been mentioned. My dermatologist had also been to a symposium for skin diseases recently, and he was aware of the connection. He even told me the Portland, Oregon VAMC was doing an extensive study on the link between PCT and hepatitis. He suggested I pursue the cause of it.

I assumed I had a case of infectious hepatitis (hepatitis A) in service. I did two tours of duty back to back over there, and I had extensive exposure to Agent Orange and Blue herbicides. Liver function tests showed there was something radically wrong as early as 1987. I reported for an Agent Orange exam at the VAMC in Tacoma that I had requested, in September 1993. It documented liver dysfunction again. The promised doctor's appointment to examine my skin never materialized. I was informed that would be scheduled soon and not to worry. I never heard back from the VAMC. I was beginning to suspect a VA pattern of delay and deny in their health field now too.

I contacted AMVETS and filed for PCT in March 1994 based either on the hepatitis or Agent Orange (AO). Bob Talbott, my AMVETS representative, was a nice guy but he was preoccupied with a desire for a new job elsewhere. Our first meet and greet consisted of a discussion of how he probably wouldn't be my rep through the whole process. After filing, I expected the standard Compensation and Pension exam dance. Nothing happened. Bob said be patient, so I went on about my business. I was now getting phlebotomies for the PCT every three weeks. For those unfamiliar with the term, a phlebotomy is like donating blood at the Red Cross, but they throw it in the trash can. The other difference was you had to pay them twenty dollars to do it. It reduced the iron in my blood that damaged my liver, but it also made me weak and anemic. The blood bank will only allow you to donate every fifty-seven days. I was going every twenty-one. After the third one I started to get a real buzz going after each one.

The magic paper arrived on November 7, 1994. VA interpreted my filing to be for (1) residuals of hepatitis and (2) PCT due *strictly* to AO. My military medical records were, as I mentioned, severely compromised as were my military records. There was no record of my service in Vietnam. I was smart and had kept records showing my travel and service there. There was nothing in my service medical records (SMRs) about hepatitis except for me checking the box on my Form 88 separation physical. Denying claims is an art form for the VA. First, they take what you file for and recharacterize it in their terms. Thus, a disease I had in service (hepatitis) was nowhere documented, and the PCT could not be associated with AO because my records said I wasn't in South Vietnam. There was no discussion of whether the PCT was related to the hepatitis because I never had hepatitis in VA's eyes. This is called divide and conquer. I wrote back to the hospital in Thailand again and requested my records of the hepatitis and my six-week stay as an inpatient. I submitted these and TDY orders to Vietnam with my Notice of Disagreement (NOD) on December 2, 1994, and waited again.

In January 1995, I received a Statement of the Case (SOC), saying they had received my new evidence. VA went on to say they would be making a decision soon and would contact me. I also attended a Compensation and Pension exam (C&P) for my tinnitus in February and began a new wait. I never heard from them again regarding any of this. In the meantime, Bob said not to worry. Sometimes it takes VA time to assemble all the evidence. He reasoned that if it was taking a lot of time, it probably meant they were finally obtaining all the records from Thailand. I settled in for a long wait as I had when they did the BVA dog and pony show in 1992. I contacted AMVETS again in January 1996, but Bob had moved on to his new calling as a used car salesman. No one there knew anything, but they promised they'd look into it and get back to me. I had other fish to fry and a family to feed. I assumed no news was bad news. Being unschooled in this process, I was unaware that VA was obligated to review my new evidence and give me an up or down decision on it. By failing to do so, the claim sat growing dust. It was still open regardless of whether VA chose to act on it. To be truthful, I simply gave up on ever seeing anything on this. AMVETS was quite obviously taking a flyer on it just as the VA had. It was becoming pretty clear to me that this was how VSOs *and* the VA operated.

Based on my new claim for hepatitis and PCT, I decided to get a more detailed examination of my liver in 1995. Extensive testing revealed a new type of hepatitis called HCV (hepatitis C virus). The doctors didn't sound any alarms. They simply mentioned that I had "antibodies" to this new disease. The negative effects on my liver were beginning to become obvious though. Fatigue and a general feeling of malaise were more frequent. Often I had nausea in the morning. I figured it had something to do with the phlebotomies.

All during the period I was working my VA claim with AMVETS, my health had been declining. I was experiencing intense abdominal cramping from early 1995 on. I lost about thirty pounds over fifteen months and finally gave in to my spouse's plea to seek medical help. It culminated on July 5, 1996, when I collapsed. My wife took me in to the emergency room, and doctors diagnosed an intestinal blockage. An operation removed a sizable part of my small bowel. The diagnosis was Crohn's disease even though the pathology report didn't reveal it. The surgeon was happy. He had suspected cancer in someone my age. At this time, there was no suggestion that this might be related to Agent Orange. Subsequent medical studies have since shown a link for this as well as ulcerative colitis. VA, as usual, staunchly denies anything tying the two together.

Following my 1996 surgery, the fatigue and sick feeling were always present. Some days were good, and some weren't. I knew something was wrong but really couldn't point to any one thing. My regular doctors were now on the warpath to get me to try the new Interferon therapy for HCV. It was untested and had a poor success rate in the early years. I reviewed all their literature and said no thanks. My PCT was under control, but I was still continuing the phlebotomies. The fatigue and anemia never abated.

I attributed most of this to old age (forty-seven). I was now running the construction crews, and the added toll of twelve-hour days was telling on me. This is where matters stood ten years later.

In 2006, my wife asked me when I last had a physical examination. I figured it was when I left the Air Force in 1973. I promptly reported in October for my fifty-fifth year checkup, and my new doctor didn't like what he saw. At his and my wife's prodding, I decided it was time to bite the bullet. When I declined the interferon therapy in 1998, the doctor didn't go into a diatribe of "You'll be sorry." In fact, he just shrugged his shoulders and moved on to suturing the damage from the nail gun to my thumb. How bad could it be? Keep reading.

Science and medicine had made great strides since 1998, and the doctors convinced me I could hack this in 2007. The game plan was to do the injection on Thursdays after work. It would be rough on Friday through Sunday afterward, but I would recover and be able to bounce back by Monday morning. The documented side effects of the interferon were explained as "flu-like aches and pains with some nausea." That was a masterpiece of understatement.

My doctor didn't tell me he was part of a testing protocol to measure the success rate of the pegylated interferon and ribavirin. I was a paying guinea pig, and they would have told me anything to get me in the program. My insurance company then announced they wouldn't cover the cost of each $750 injection. We agreed to do it nevertheless. Life was more important than money and sure death.

I did all the preparatory baseline testing and had a liver biopsy. It wasn't good. My liver was 75 percent gone. The PCT was making things worse. The good news was that the HCV was genotype 3A, which was very responsive to the new interferon regimen. I was told that treatment would be twenty-six weeks, and chances of remission were 80 percent. My doctor overlooked one thing. I had an autoimmune disease on record

(Crohn's), and my antinuclear antibody test showed 160:1, which is definitely elevated.

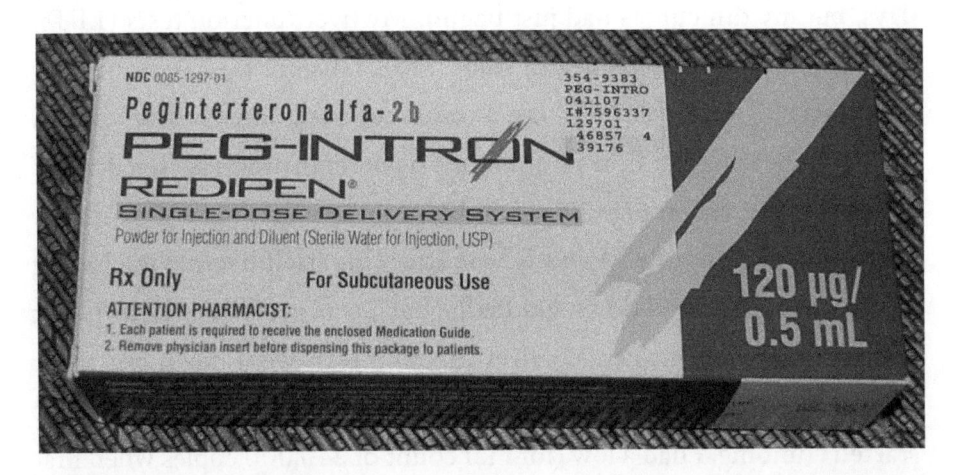

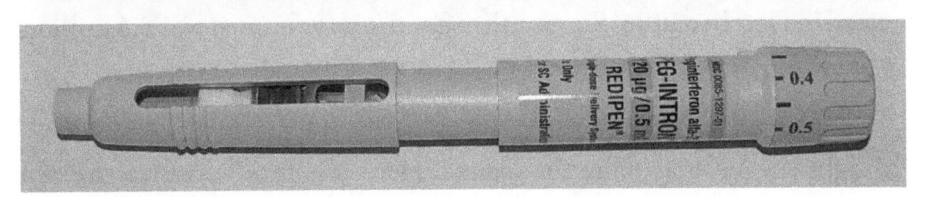

Interferon and autoimmune issues are like grease and fire. Imagine throwing napalm on a fully engulfed house fire. That is exactly what happened. The problem was they couldn't put the fire out afterward.

My first (and last) interferon shot was April 12, 2007. Within four hours I was nauseous, fevered, and disoriented. I drove home from work at twenty-five miles per hour in a forty five mile-per-hour zone with cars honking behind me. It was seventy-five outside, yet I had the heater on full blast and was freezing. I was so cold I sat in my van for forty-five minutes, trying to get warm enough to make a break for the back door. I crawled into bed, pulled two blankets on, and began to shake. My wife came home several hours later, and we just figured this was what interferon was all about. I ate a couple of ibuprofen and drifted off. By 9:00 p.m., my temperature was 102 and still climbing. Six more ibuprofen didn't touch it. It began to recede from 104.5 at 11:30 p.m. as my wife was preparing to haul me off to the emergency room. I recovered over the next several days, but my difficulties had just begun. My liver function tests (LFTs) started to climb, and my health went into a tailspin. By November, my ALT (SGPT) was over 600. The antinuclear antibodies test revealed a 1:2510, indicating a radical autoimmune disorder in progress. The doctors decided to put me on prednisone and Imuran in hopes of turning off the autoimmune response. My body was attacking itself like a dog chasing its tail. Things slowed down gradually, but I was never the same. I kept getting sicker and weaker. My liver function tests went down but never returned to the pre-interferon levels. Meanwhile, my HCV viral count started climbing. I had a low (for me) count of 240,000 copies when first tested in October 2006. Six months after the interferon, it was 8.5 million. A year later, it had gradually dropped to 3.5 million.

When we discovered the damage from the HCV, we made plans to fight the VA and refile the claims. Here was proof-positive that the healed disease in service was far worse. The plan was to accumulate all the information and medical records and file them with VA after we had the proof.

In November 2006, I contacted the Military Order of the Purple Heart (MOPH) and notified them of my plans. We started again February 23, 2007, as a reopening of the 1994 claim. VA's initial letter sounded like they had never received any of the new evidence I submitted in December 1994, so I resubmitted all that again. I also submitted all the medical records I had from the private doctors showing the biopsy and brief interferon therapy. I reported once again for a tinnitus exam in June 2007. VA instantly granted me 10 percent all the way back to 1994. What was this all about? I now knew something that should have happened thirteen years ago was suddenly "fixed." There was no explanation for why they decided to give me the back pay. It was simply a rating and a check for about $15K. My representative, Pat, from MOPH never asked why they chose an effective date of 1994 on this either. By rights, the claim date should have been the newer February 2007 filing date... unless there was a mistake.

In October of 2007, I called up the MOPH and asked for a progress report on the hepatitis and the PCT claim. My representative told me I could call VA's 800 number for an update. This was what I *thought* I had hired them to do. The VA technician who answered indicated the claim had been closed out in June when the tinnitus was granted. He promised to straighten it out. Several days later, I received a new packet with the Risk Factors Questionnaire and other literature saying they were opening this as a brand new claim. It took me several weeks to get them to admit it was the old one from eight months earlier. MOPH was AWOL on this. When they did finally become involved a month later, it was already fixed. I started to have second thoughts about VSOs again. I was becoming more ill by the day and getting little or no help from them.

In hopes of learning more about the VA claims process, I asked my wife to get me started on computers. I had built houses for thirty-five years and had no time before this to learn. After about a month, I felt sick, but not from the hepatitis. There was so much the MOPH representative *wasn't* telling me about how this system worked. I guess Veterans were expected to figure a lot of this out by themselves. I accidentally discovered the need for a doctor's nexus letter in January 2008. I kept seeing references to it in Board of Veterans Appeals (BVA) decisions. It was obvious that Vets who had a nexus won and those without didn't. I promptly contacted my hepatologist, and he agreed to write one.

On my next MOPH visit a month later, I brought up this subject. I handed the representative, Pat, a copy of the nexus for his records and mentioned I had sent in a statement about my injury/transfusion. Pat was furious. He said it was common knowledge that Veterans had to have one (a nexus). *Everyone* knew that. At this appointment, Pat also informed me that chances of winning a hepatitis/PCT claim were zero. People with hepatitis usually got it from drug abuse. PCT had to be evident within twelve months of leaving Vietnam, period. Tattoos were willful misconduct, and I couldn't win with them. I don't have any tattoos. In summary, Pat wanted me to abandon the claim. I now know why. Everybody wants a winning team record, and MOPH was no different. Taking on cases that are impossible to win is futile and drags down the win/loss ratio. It's bad PR for business. I had won the tinnitus, and I should go home happy. I had been doing serious research on my claims, and I knew tattoos and STDs were not willful misconduct despite what Pat said. This was beginning to look and smell like the Disabled American Veterans fiasco of 1989. I had won the tinnitus, so I should have been happy and gone home. Wrong.

I mentioned that I was very sick and unable to work at this appointment. Pat promptly handed me a Form 21-8940. This is a claim form for Total Disability. He knew I didn't qualify for it but offered it anyway. I pointed out the futility in claiming it. He was getting irritated that I seemed to be familiar with the inside of the benefits manual. He wanted this conversation over and me out of his office pronto. He handed me his copy of the Code of Federal Regulations (CFRs) and said, "If you're so knowledgeable about all of this, then maybe you don't need me. And while we're on the subject, let's get something perfectly clear. If you file anything else with the VA without going through me, we'll discontinue your representation."

My wife had been there with me on that visit. She was appalled to think that this was the legal team I was hanging my hopes on. Her feeling was that we stood a better chance of winning the Publisher's Clearinghouse Sweepstakes. We went home and talked about it. The next day, we made the decision to go it alone. I filed a letter with VA withdrawing the MOPH power of attorney and said I'd represent myself. This was an important decision. If I had lost, we'd be stuck with them all the way through an appeal in DC. After the DAV disaster in 1992, we decided that would be dumb. We analyzed all that we had and went over what had been submitted. I filed more supporting information as I found it and finally rested my case in March 2008.

I had searched for the pilot I flew with for a buddy letter regarding my wound. He was dead. He was killed in an aircraft accident while I was in the hospital with the hepatitis. Things were looking pretty dim. VA sent me out for a C&P in March 2008 and asked for my medical records from the private doctors. Apparently, they had "misplaced" them, or MOPH hadn't sent them in. I drove the records to Seattle that day. VA still wasn't happy, so they sent out for an Independent Medical Opinion (IMO) on me. I simply didn't understand this. I had private records from Thailand showing hepatitis during service. I had the magic nexus letter, and I had a documented case of HCV. These were the three things I needed. VA didn't believe me. VA's Independent Medical Opinion backfired and came back in my favor in May.

I was granted service connection on June 1, of 2008 at 100 percent. VA promptly dropped the PCT claim in the trash again as they had earlier. On September 29, I called them up on the 800 number and discovered this. On October 2, the PCT rating arrived in the mail. I looked at all the evidence and decided to appeal for an earlier effective date (EED) of March 1994 because I suspected VA had never finished the old claims. I don't need to tell you that this went over like screen doors in submarines. VA finally said that the reason I didn't get the tinnitus rating in 1994 was that there had been an "unresolved disagreement" that prevented it, but that VA had rectified the problem. Their attitude was that they had made good on it so there really was no issue outstanding. VA's legal rationale for this is, "Justice delayed is not justice denied."

April 24, 2009, dawned, and my Crohn's symptoms returned. It had been in remission for twelve years. The interferon woke it up, and it came back with a vengeance. I had let my regular medical insurance expire because I now had "free" VA medical. This was a major error. Free anything should be examined closely like the inside of a horse's mouth. I had gone to my local hospital with the permission of the VA and had been admitted. The next day, the VA meat wagon showed up and hauled me up to Seattle. They fooled around for a day or two and finally did surgery on me on the twenty-seventh. Things looked good for a few more days, and then all hell broke loose. I began to swell like a beach ball. Everything swelled up down there. Then my brains departed. The doctors delayed for a week until I was almost comatose. They called my wife and said I was being combative and delusional. She showed up and prepared to have me moved to another hospital May 2. That got some action. A new surgeon showed up and immediately scheduled me for another surgery an hour later. Something was wrong, and VA finally decided to go back in and find out what. It was ugly. They botched sewing up the intestine, and it had been leaking for a week. Sepsis had set in, and the peritonitis was extensive. The doctors said

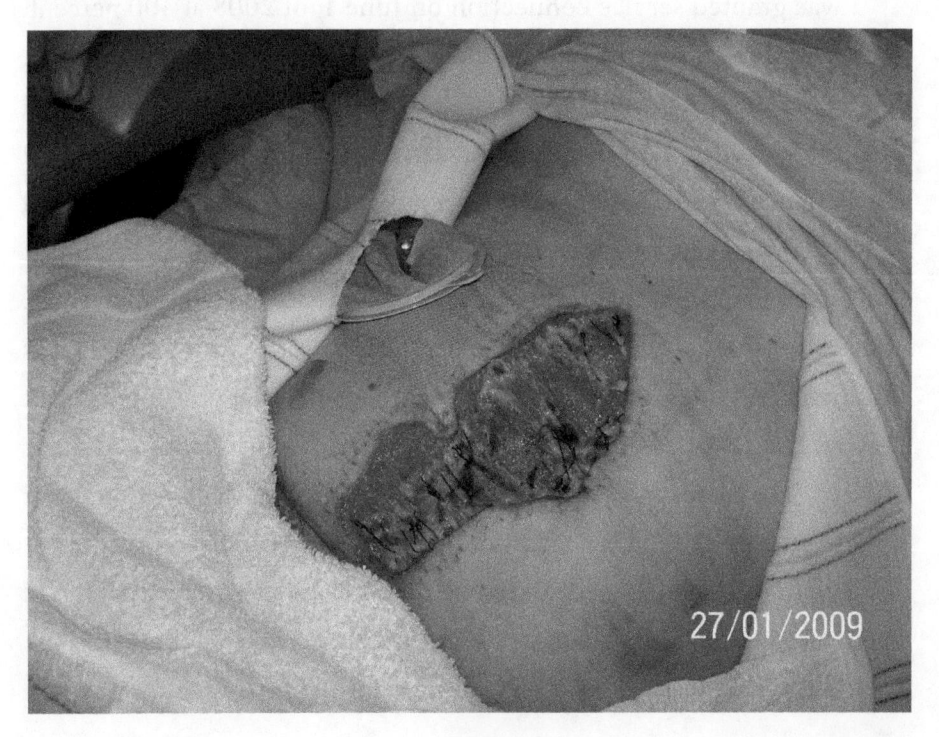

I probably wouldn't make it. They gave me a colostomy to allow the abdominal cavity to recuperate. I spent the next month in ICU. My Father's Day present from VA was MRSA. In late October, the nurse accidentally overdosed me on Coumadin blood thinner. I received two units of blood in the night and read about it a year later. For Veterans Day, VA graciously gave me a heart attack from all the blood clots developing in my inferior vena cava. I had several more laparoscopic procedures to clean up intractable pockets of infection through October/November. They released me to go home just before Christmas 2009.

I returned in March 2010 to take down the colostomy and rejoin my bowel. The preoperational EEG exam March 11 revealed the November 2009 heart attack. They proceeded to surgery on March 15 anyway. I was excited about returning to "normal." Everything seemed to be going well. I felt better, and the healing process had begun. I was started on a liquid diet and was thinking BACON and eggs. The idea of a bowel movement after eleven months even sounded exciting. Seriously. It had been that long.

March 21 dawned, and I got permission to go on a regular diet. My new surgery immediately started leaking feces out of my former colostomy site. To say the surgeon was pissed is a masterpiece of understatement. They threw me on a gurney, and off to the operating room we went for the fourth time. I was informed I was probably going to wake up with a new, permanent colostomy bag. I suggested using a needle and lots of thread this time, since the *last two* she'd supervised didn't hold up very well. To my immense relief, when I did recover consciousness, there was no bag. The surgeon had pulled the same stunt back in April 2009—she failed to put enough stitches and staples in to hold it together. I'm no surgeon, but I built houses for a living. An extra nail or two won't get you in trouble with the building inspector. Thread and staples are way more expensive and time-consuming than nails, apparently.

VA released me in late April 2010. I was so weak, I couldn't climb up steps. I weighed 118 pounds and barely remembered my name and DOB. I was too weak to work on my claims for several months. Trying to gain weight was impossible. I was dehydrated and required regular IV infusions of fluid to avoid being readmitted to the hospital. By June, I had enough strength to resume my claims battle.

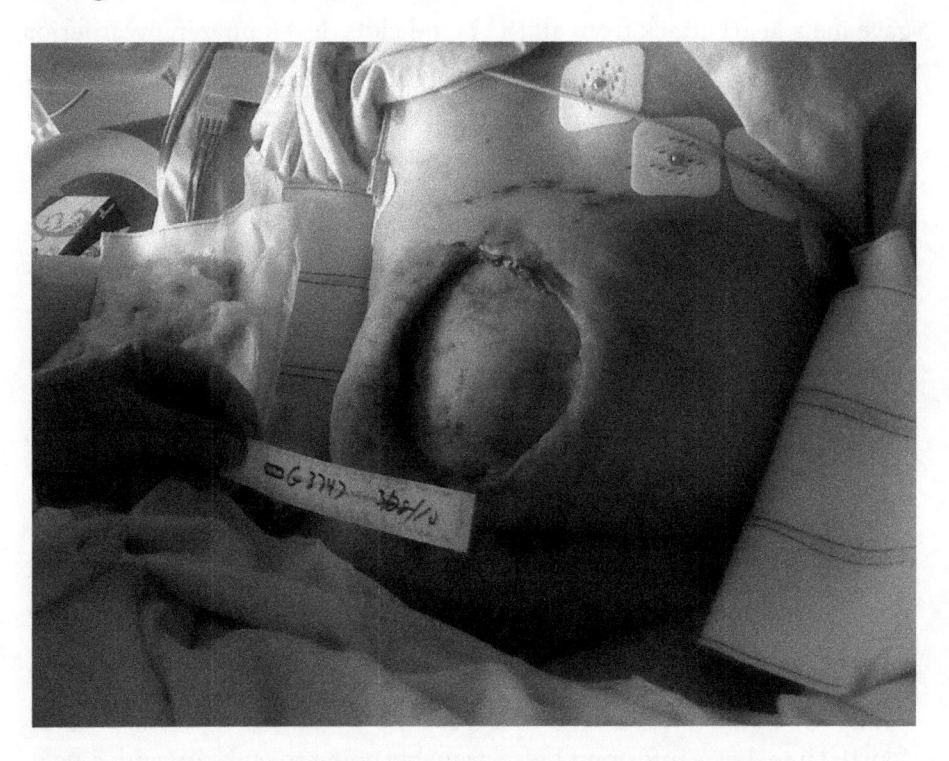

I had filed a lot of letters contesting VA's refusal to give me an earlier date. I put in a lot of reasons as I discovered them in the Board of Veterans Appeals (BVA) decisions I was reading daily. They never answered me. Finally, to protect myself, I filed Form 9s for all three claims. That got their attention. The first letter back was a formal SOC for the tinnitus explaining why they weren't going back to my 1989 filing. I had figured if they went back to 1994, that maybe I could roll them for an earlier date. No dice. They did make the error of saying the tinnitus claim was granted because there was a "disagreement" still on the books in 1995. The next letter was one to inform me that I couldn't file Form 9s until I had officially received SOCs. The hepatitis SOC showed up a week after the tinnitus one.

As for the hepatitis, the argument against an earlier date became more humorous. VA tried to imply I hadn't submitted any new evidence and failed to file a Form 9 in 1994. That was their "post hoc rationalization." The truth is they didn't *know* what happened in 1994 because they never finished the claim. They were attempting to reconstruct my past claims history based on what they should have done, not on what they didn't do. In order to avoid paying, they started building a story around the few facts that were there. In their eyes, it was my fault.

VA had received my Notice of Disagreement with the PCT rating decision in October 2008. On March 29, 2010, they upped my rating to 40 percent to account for the phlebotomies. They still refused to grant an earlier date. They reasoned that VA couldn't review the new evidence in 1994 until I had signed and returned my Form 9. No Form 9 equaled claim not appealed. They said proof of being in Vietnam wasn't proof of PCT from Agent Orange. VA had now presented three different theories over a year of why I was not going to get an earlier date. If this were the case, they should have never given me the tinnitus back to 1994.

I had my board hearing at the Seattle Regional Office in April 2011. I think it went well, but then again I thought things were going pretty cool back in July of 1990 when I had my regional office hearing about my back. I will not be shocked to hear they want to fight me over this to the Court of Veterans Appeals. The back pay will not come cheaply. I know my case is airtight, but to the VA, that means nothing. I have also filed to reopen my back claim based on clear and unmistakable error (CUE). This will also cost them if I win. They should have granted it and the hepatitis when I filed way back when. They would have gotten off far cheaper. Now I'm pissed and know how to play the game.

If this wasn't a sad tale, I found out they used cadaver skin to cover up my abdomen and diaphragm on the last operation. They had done so many surgeries by now, they'd run out of skin. The product is called Alloderm and was recalled in 2007. VA must use up its old supplies before they buy newer stuff. The nurses issued me an abdominal support (men's girdle) when I was discharged. I was given a lifting limit of 15 pounds—permanently. The hernias started blooming about four months later. They refuse to this day to cut me open again to fix it. I'm actually okay with that. I wear the belt and am a little leery of going near any VAMC for surgery ever again. Their success rate on me is one for four. I continue to recover and watch my hernias bloom like flowers. I now have something called short bowel syndrome too. VA managed to remove quite a bit of my small intestine over the course of the four surgeries. My health appears to have returned now that I'm over the Interferon misadventure. My AST/ALT kept going up and spiked in June 2011. I was forced to change my eating habits. Giving up red meat was harder to do than cigarettes. The short

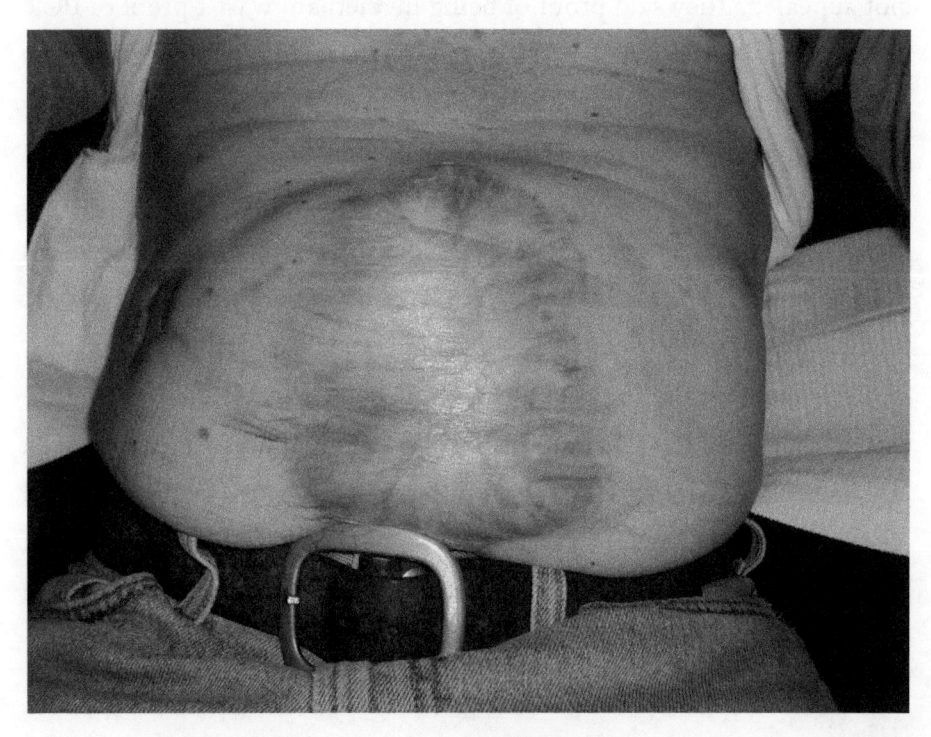

bowel disorder has caused me to revamp my life. Every disease has its ups and downs. Mine seems to be getting worse right now. In addition, a disease called cryoglobulinemia is coming back. It began after the interferon and is starting up again.

This is the history of my claims over the last twenty-three years. This book will attempt to teach you how to win from what I have learned.

# C
## History of VA Claims Process

It is not necessary to know the why and how of the VA's history, but it will give you insight on their thinking processes. Why you have so much difficulty getting action or a sympathetic ear has much to do with what you are filing for. Obviously, the two hardest claims to win are HCV and PTSD; the former for its hidden nature of surfacing thirty years later, and PTSD because it is a mental issue. Doctors cannot see into your head to measure the ring of tinnitus, nor can they measure bent brain syndrome. These are self-reported criteria. With PTSD, certain things are indicators—like when you have uncontrolled anger, poor hygiene, and no friends. A poor jobs record can be a dead giveaway. VA says that some Vets are incredibly lazy and hate to work. The VA gravy train of $3,000 a month can be very appealing to those who have no advanced training or specialized skills. Some Veterans' economic futures are rather bleak. Seeing other Vets succeed in winning compensation from the government simply makes them try to do the same.

I don't intend to insult Veterans who legitimately suffer from PTSD. I know about it. I did two tours back to back from May 1970 to May 1972. When I came home, a car backfiring was all it took for me to jump into a ditch. In fact, the sound of a chopper flying over can still queer me for the whole day. I would say that with proper psychiatric help, this condition can be overcome. I never had any and seem to have recovered. My family doesn't always think so. I suspect lots of time heals all wounds. Veterans of WW2 had it far worse than my generation in Vietnam. A great majority managed to overcome their mental trauma; and most, but not all, went on to lead productive lives. Historians attribute this to WW2 Vets only engaging in combat forty or so days a year. Vietnam combat Vets did it, on average, for 240 of their 365 days in country. VA showed no inclination to grant service connection for this after the Vietnam war, so many never bothered to apply. In fact, the military went out of their way to write it up as personality disorders. The reason is simple. Personality disorders are characterized as defects that were there before you signed up. They just didn't materialize *until* you were in the service. VA doesn't pay for disease or injury that preceded service so the Catch 22 kicks in. PTSD was "invented" in 1981 as far as the Vietnam Vets were concerned. The war had been over for six years by then—just long enough for everyone to forget. It would be another twenty years before the chickens came home to roost.

The Vietnam era produced a large number of PTSD cases with more filings daily. I suspect this is a product of a defective economy that brings out a bunch of Johnny come latelys. It stands to reason that if your brain was bent in 1967 from combat, that you would seek out mental health counseling before 2012 to correct it. This isn't what I am trying to teach here. It merely looks at one facet of service connection that may help you decide what your future with VA is. If your records show combat and a sufficient stressor can be proven, you will eventually prevail. Your doctors will have to say as much too. However, VA has begun to make it more difficult. As of 2010, they use *only* their doctors to make the decision. You can still have your own private psychiatrist write a nexus letter, but the VA is going to rely heavily on their own medical specialists. Rather convenient, huh?

Veterans have been filing claims for almost two hundred years, going back to the war of 1812. Pensions for both the armies of the North and South were awarded after the War of Northern Aggression concluded in 1865. Everyone remembers the words of President Abraham Lincoln at Gettysburg, and VA has even appropriated them for its logo. How tacky and opportunistic can you get? Promise Vets Arpêge Perfume and give them WD-40 eau d'stress.

VA was faced with a dilemma after WW2 and had to rethink their strategy. The number of injured were overwhelming the system, and the claims were legitimate. They set out to increase the hospital system they had started after the First World War. The requirements for service connection and compensation were tightened up to prevent a rush to the trough for benefits. The Korean War didn't increase numbers dramatically, and everything settled down for a decade until the beginning of the Vietnam conflict.

This war brought a new aircraft into play. With the advent of the helicopter, not only could vast numbers of troops be moved into battle in short order, but the gravely wounded could also be evacuated rapidly to rear echelon medical facilities. The survival rate went up dramatically, and the severity of the survived injuries multiplied. VA was not prepared for this new influx. It started to overwhelm the VA medical system.

VA instituted a new idea utilizing Boards consisting of three judges each to hear appeals in the early sixties. These boards consisted of one doctor/judge on them to help speed up decisions without requiring additional development and remands. It not only helped expedite many a claim but also was arbitrary. Veterans with valid claims who had no way to document them were denied regularly with no avenue for appeal. Additionally, the National Personnel Records Center in St. Louis, Missouri, had a fire in 1973 that destroyed many Korean-era records. This wiped out those claims and prevented any new ones for the guys who lost their records. The government was tasked with being the keeper of the information, and they couldn't even be bothered to install a sprinkler system or smoke alarms. Brilliant.

The Board of Veterans Appeals continued on with no supervision for thirty plus years until 1988. Congress, at the urging of many upset Vets and their congressional representatives, finally voted in a new level of appeals review. The Court of Veterans Appeals (COVA or the Court)) opened in 1989. This finally allowed Vets access to the higher courts that other citizens have always enjoyed. Unfortunately, the VA didn't want to change its old ways. They had done business their way for over a century. They resisted this by pretending nothing had changed. Bad vibes between the Court and the VA secretary continue to this day. In 1994, the BVA started a policy where a single judge would constitute a "Board," thus freeing up more judges to decide claims. The Court had by now struck down the practice of judges playing doctor. The old doctor/judges were allowed to retire as they reached the twenty-year mark, and no new ones were hired. The VA still has the same number (sixty) of Veterans Law Judges (VLJs) as they did then. They have an additional crop of new ones in training called acting VLJs. These judges in the wings are allowed to decide claims up to ninety days at a time on a temporary basis.

The VA system of adjudication, for you newbies, is not all that complex. VA utilizes a system called ex parte justice. This is lawspeak for a technique whereby you submit all your evidence and wait. VA collects your medical records and any private ones you have identified to them for retrieval and makes a decision. There is no Perry Mason trial with opposing attorneys. It is more like a large insurance company that you submit a claim to. If they deny, you are given a year to submit new evidence to contest their findings. If the claim is still in contention after this, an appeal is initiated and the case moves to Washington DC and the Board of Veterans Appeals (BVA). You are assigned a docket date based on the order of which it was received and you await your turn. This too is in the form of ex parte justice. You are free to submit even more argument and evidence and waive review of it in the first instance by the Regional Office (RO or VARO). This allows your case to be heard sooner at the BVA without remand back to your local office. A denial at the BVA is not the end. With the advent of the Court of Appeals for Veterans Claims (CAVC), you now can appeal higher. The CAVC is not part of the Veterans Administration. It is a stand-alone Court and provides much better justice to Vets. I don't mean to imply that there is none at the lower tribunals. They are, however, full of errors and don't care about it. The Board of Veterans Appeals is run by the VA Secretary, so it isn't independent like Social Security judges. The 60 percent remand rate from the Court is pretty solid evidence that justice is spotty at these lower levels. This book will be instrumental to you to achieve that which many say is impossible—winning at this. Not only winning, but winning at a local level rather than having a time-consuming appeal.

A loss before the Court of Veterans Appeals is not the end of the road. You can appeal this denial to the Federal Circuit and seek to have it reversed there. The avenue to the Supreme Court obviously is there as well. Obtaining certiorari for this is rare, though not impossible. If the VA secretary loses at the Court of Veterans Appeals, he has the right to file for reversal at the Federal Circuit as well as the Supreme Court. This occurs, but only rarely.

# CHAPTER 2

## BEGINNING THE PROCESS

### A
### VSO Representatives

**Things needed:** http://www.rattler-firebird.org/va/forms/22a.pdf
VA Form 21-22, Appointment of Individual as Claimant's Representative (Power of Attorney, or POA). You must fill out this hall pass in order to even talk to a VSO. It's like a Miranda warning, and you say, "Yes. I understand I'm preparing to get my teeth kicked in." Ignore this if you intend to represent yourself.

When you decide it is time to file your claim, there is an orderly process to follow. Many seek out the services of Veterans Services Organizations (VSOs). These come in all different sizes and flavors ranging from state- and county-sponsored representatives to the nationally recognized ones. The last time I checked, there were forty-six of them, but the figure isn't static. Some discontinued this function like the American Red Cross in the early nineties. Newer ones such as the Vietnam Veterans of America (VVA) have replaced them. Some states have *no* Veterans organizations to help us. Each state is different, so be careful. Congress has specified that no attorneys can be involved in this at the lowest levels. We have two choices—VSOs or going at it alone by ourselves (pro se). Since it is an ex parte legal process, there isn't much lawyering involved in it. You will not need Black's Law book to proceed. Ex parte is lawspeak for "one party only." It's no more complicated than filing for a fender bender with Allstate. In fact, a Veteran is given far more protections than in a civilian setting. Getting justice seems to be the problem.

Choosing a VSO as your representative has benefits and liabilities. No two are alike, and their officers can be brilliant or dumb as a goat. You have absolutely no control over who you will draw. Some are extremely well educated in the process and will serve you well. Others treat it as a nine-to-five proposition and would prefer to be out fishing or watching basketball. The VSO will be the interface between you and the VA. You need them to be your mailman and an outlet for information. While you can call the VA for an update on your claim or utilize the new Ebenefits website (www.ebenefits.va.gov/ebenefits-portal/ebenefits.portal ) to watch the progress, the VSO will still be the one who ultimately contacts you with the results. Of course, the VA notifies you too—about two weeks later. Your VSO can make decisions without asking you. This is not always good. They may agree to a rump settlement.

If you appeal a denied decision with the VSO as your legal representative, you must use them all the way through to the next appellate level. You cannot jump ship in midstream. Your next opportunity to get rid of them will be when you choose to appeal to the Court of Veterans Appeals (Court). This can have interesting consequences. Some Vets I have helped have given up in frustration and have taken over their claims without being obvious about it. What is the VSO going to do? Fire *you*? This gets comical when you win and your long-lost representative you haven't spoken to in several years calls up and wants to do a photo op with you for their trophy wall. I have heard of two.

The Disabled American Veterans Organization, which is the largest in the business, is usually the one most Vets turn to. I did the first time.

All VSOs will refuse to help you until you sign a VA Form 21-22 Power of Attorney (POA). This grants them funds from the VA for helping you (some will dispute this). I asked the lady who answers the phone at the Washington State Department of Veterans Affairs. She says yes, but VA pays very little. Once the POA is signed, that's the end of many an involved representative. They are so driven to produce new POAs that your case is lost in the shuffle. When you arrive for an appointment and the rep stares at you blankly and cannot remember who you are and what you're claiming, you realize your legal strategy may be compromised.

You should know that by letting the VSO be your representative, you are allowing them the authority to do whatever they think is best without even consulting you. I would never put my fate in their hands, based on that alone. This can get scary on appeal to DC. My DAV representative never pointed out all the errors in the RO decision. He just pleaded for leniency and benefit of the doubt. He did this with no input from me. I was unaware of any of this until I got my copy of the C-file and found it eighteen years later.

# B
# Going at It Alone Pro Se

**Things Needed:** VA Form 21-526 or file with all the information requested on that form. http://www.rattler-firebird.org/va/forms/21-526.pdf

As a personal matter, in this one instance, I believe it's smarter to use the form to file than using 8.5 x 11 paper. VA manages to screw so much up anyway that it hardly pays to torture them on this one. If it helps you get the dependency issues over sooner, then it might be advised. VA had my info and still made me produce every bit of it again twenty years later. I checked, and it was still in the C-file, but they didn't look.

This includes DD-214, marriage or divorce records; birth certificates for dependents; SSNs for dependents; certified copies of Veteran's former marriage or divorce records and SSNs of ex-wives (all of them).

When to submit: At the time of submission with claim.

## Pro Se Representation

Let's look at the second choice that I like. I have done this three times—each with a VSO. The track record is spotty. DAV got me 0 percent for tinnitus and hearing in 1992 and acted like "we" had just hit the Powerball lottery. I didn't share my representative's excitement. I lost the important claim for my back, and the decision was extremely flawed. Because they (and I) had no legal training, I never noticed this until I studied VA's legal process and spotted it myself. My representative never even hinted that I could appeal this further up the chain to the newly minted COVA (now the CAVC).

My second outing was with the AMVETS VSO. They are just as stand up as the next outfit but have a bar and a restaurant at their offices. Booze won't improve your odds—just your outlook. AMVETS filed my claims for hepatitis, PCT, and an increase for my tinnitus. DAV never told me that I could file for an increase, so I never did. The representative, in search of more POA victims, was very difficult to reach once the magic paper had been submitted. I saw him one last time in November of 1994 when I filed my NOD with my denial for these claims. He left the organization shortly after to become a used car salesman. VA never completed my claim, and that is part of the story I will tell later on.

I filed in February of 2007 with the Military Order of the Purple Heart(MOPH) because my friend Lars did. He told me these guys were on the ball and involved 100 percent. He lied. MOPH was marginally better and accessible, but they suffer the same problem of all VSOs. They simply have no legal training. You would have the same luck with your claim if you depended on your next-door neighbor. Fortunately for me, my wife realized this on the third try, and we decided to bail out and go it alone. It made sense after having no luck with prior VSOs. Lars never did win and died two years later from pancreatic cancer.

With that behind us, let's look at what's behind door number 2. Representing yourself has many tactical advantages. You have no one to blame but yourself if things go south. Using this method, there really isn't much to worry about other than time limits. You can purchase a calendar and accomplish this as well or better than your VSO. All the decisions will come to you as long as you keep your address current and are not in the habit of moving every three months. If you are footloose, I strongly suggest an anchor address such as your parents or a PO Box. This is critical where time limits are concerned. You cannot legitimately use the "I moved and didn't get it" excuse. VA's return excuse will be "Sorry. You didn't tell us you moved. If you had, we could have notified you." This can be crucial if you are homeless, and your zip code changes with the seasons.

Representing yourself frees you of depending on the legal capabilities of the chuckleheads you appoint to help you. I strongly suggest you be of reasonable intelligence to even contemplate this by yourself. If you are totally engrossed in a job with a big dose of family, this may not fit in. Using a VSO may be the ticket, but it will require constant supervision. If you are advanced in years and an empty nester type, this will fit in nicely as an evening pastime. With the Internet, access to all manner of information is at your fingertips. Your need to depend on others is only limited by your computer talents.

VA would have you believe that everything must be presented on their stationery and forms. Hogwash. I have never used anything more than what I call the Standard Form 8.5 x 11, also known as computer paper. As long as you identify yourself sufficiently, VA can figure it out from there. When you file your original correspondence with them, I might suggest you use their 21-526 because it has all the requests they will want for information about dependents. Or you can download the form, figure out what they want, and revert back to the SF 8.5 x 11. I dislike them so much I use regular paper exclusively. It makes no difference. There is also the new VONAPP process whereby you can file electronically. Oddly, VA took all my information on my dependents in 1989, and I still had a long uphill battle when I finally won in 2008. It was as if they had never received it in the first place so what's the point? The same happened with my spouse. I had to resubmit my marriage licenses all over again and my divorce decree.

The VA will never tell you this, but a Vet who represents him/herself is accorded kid gloves treatment. The reason for this is simple. Later on, after the inevitable denial (if there is one), VA does not want to be perceived as being the big ogre Goliath who struck down David. This is bad PR and newspapers love these underdog stories. To avoid this, VA bends over backward where they might not when you are represented by a VSO. They reason that a VSO knows what they're doing, and if they screw up, well, tough luck for you. Similarly, at the BVA level, the Vet must be made to feel as though he/she is in a claimant-friendly environment where every benefit is accorded. No trickery is allowed. There will be "gotcha" moments, but they will be yours, not VA's. Just follow the advice here. If you have to go up to the CAVC, they really give you the royal treatment. A smart Vet will get a lawyer for the CAVC though. I would.

If you are denied at the regional level, you will finally be allowed access to real legal help at your own expense. You may now have a lawyer; and he is entitled to 20 percent, and no more, of any winnings. They are often difficult to obtain if your potential settlement is peanuts. However, if this is a jackpot that has been growing like a progressive Las Vegas slot for eight years, you'll have no trouble finding one. A smart Vet with a strong case probably doesn't need a lawyer anyway. A long battle is often the product of a gross procedural error or the absence of critical evidence that would prove the case. There are exceptions to any rule, and I will show you some as we get deeper into this.

A lawyer also may utilize the Equal Access to Justice Act (EAJA) and collect for a fixed number of billing hours directly to the VA in the event of a remand where you are justified. He only gets paid the 20 percent if you prevail. You may take him all the way to the Supreme Court if he is licensed to practice there. Most lawyers admitted to the CAVC are not at the Federal Circuit or the Supreme Court. If you go higher you may have to get another, different one. The fee is still 20%. Most attorneys add reasonable expenses to that otherwise the small amount they make wouldn't even pencil out to a profit.

# C
## Getting Your Records

**Things Needed:** SF-180 Request pertaining to Military Records (http://www.rattler-firebird.org/va/forms/180.pdf). In addition, if you have ever filed with VA for anything, you will need your complete C-File. VA always goes to St. Louis and gets your service medical records (SMRs) but leaves the rest there like the military records. You will want your SMRs so you need to file a request for the C-File. You can download one of these hummers at http://www.hughcox.com/C-FILE_req.pdf.

In addition, if you need the SF180 (http://www.archives.gov/st-louis/military-personnel/public/).

When you ask for the NPRC records, ask for everything—medical, military, etc. There is much to see in a military file. It's best if you know what's in there. A UCMJ violation for AWOL or drug bust is always a surprise later on. After a number of years we forget those.

I will assume you have begun this process and have now received both your military and medical records from St. Louis. If not, it's time for you to start there. There is a new avenue on line called Evetrecs, and the link is http://www.archives.gov/veterans/military-service-records/index.html.

Get those records and put them in a safe place. VA tends to lose things. If they don't lose them, they misplace them. Occasionally, they shred them accidentally. The National Personnel Records Center (NPRC) isn't much better. They had a big fire there in 1973. That finally convinced them to put in sprinkler systems and smoke alarms. A whole generation of Korean War Vets lost out to that brain fart. Some self-help sites will suggest you have the VA obtain the records and then file a Freedom of Information Act (FOIA) to obtain them. Bad idea. Here's why. In 1989, the VA obtained my service medical records (SMRs) and associated them with my C-File. They got the only set from St. Louis. Nowadays, St. Louis keeps the originals there and makes copies for the VA. I was lucky VA didn't lose them. I have a Vet currently who was granted SC in San Diego for rheumatoid arthritis in the late '80s. He recently filed for HCV, and VARO San Diego hasn't a clue where his C-file is. He's screwed to say the least. Get the records and put them in a safe, fireproof place.

# D
# What Records?

Okay, so what happens when St. Louis writes back and says, "What records?" Sometimes they get left behind in a hospital at your last duty station where you separated. Sometimes the SSN is scrambled, or there is some discrepancy on your birth date. I have seen many errors that create this deficiency. I advocate contacting your congressman/senator and lighting a fire under their ass. Most Vets I know have had reasonable success doing this. I also suggest you Google the last base where you were stationed prior to separation and ask their hospital records section to look through their files.

Obviously there are some of you out there who will be left out of this. I have no fix for it when it happens other than going back to your last base. They will never throw them out, but it may delay things a while. Proceeding without them is dumb. How can you defend yourself without any evidence you were even in the service? VA hasn't explained that one yet. The regulations say that you should be accorded "special treatment" if the records can't be found. All I have seen is "special denials" when this happens. If you were injured and sought medical help, it will be in those records, and getting them is very important to winning. VA will never just "take your word for it."

If you have filed before at a different VARO in the past, your C-file should be located there. You must inform VA of this so they will know to contact that VARO and have them forwarded.

# CHAPTER 3

## THE RECIPE—FILING A CLAIM

## A
## Dos and Don'ts

**Things Needed:** Buddy letters; statements from spouse, children, or parents supporting claim; pertinent private medical files from your doctors; any medical articles that support your contentions (jet guns). Obtaining stressor(s) information.
VA Form: 21-4138 Statement of Claim. VA likes it if you use this form. I don't. I personalize mine with Standard Form 8.5 x 11 (white).

Filing a claim is more than sending in the paper. You have to defend your claim by proving it. This may be easy if the evidence is in your medical records. The Court has often proclaimed that this is a two-way street. You must be involved and prove it happened the way you say it did. You must submit evidence sufficient to convince the VA examiners that you are entitled to this. Simply throwing the hand grenade at them doesn't guarantee anything. You will need three things to succeed. The first is elementary—a disease or injury that is currently active. The second has many ifs. If you had the ailment in service or a presumption of exposure to it, that will work. A recognized risk factor that could have led to it is okay too. The third leg of this stool is a nexus letter that ties this illness/injury to the one in service. This letter must be authored, at a minimum, by an ARNP, a PA, or preferably by an MD. There are other requirements necessary, and we'll discuss that in another chapter. You would be surprised at how many Vets try to file without even the first requirement. Your reason for filing is because you're ill and can prove it happened in the service. These three requirements are variously called the Caluza triangle, the Hickson elements and now the Shedden requirements.

On this subject, another requirement will arise. Some will file for a disease they had in service, which is acute such as hepatitis A or B. If they have resolved, you now have natural immunity to them much like smallpox. Filing for these is a waste of time. If you don't suffer from them now, you obviously are not bothered by them. Always remember that a claim is based on an *active* problem, not an old one that *may* become one.

### Listing the Causes

On my Web site (asknod.org), I counsel Vets to try to frame as clearly as possible what it is they think caused their disease/injury on the front page. This sheet of paper will have more French fry grease and catsup stains on it than any other in your file. For instance, in a PTSD claim, it would be obvious. The sapper attack or a horrible sexual assault would be the premiere event. For a back injury, it might have been autorotating down in a crippled Huey with a hard landing that bent the skids. For an HCV claim, it might be the genotype of the disease that ties it to Southeast Asia (SEA) exclusively (3a). The important thing I'm saying is to get this glaring fact on the front sheet of the claim. This piece of paper is going to be read and reread by each succeeding rater or supervisor. If the facts are buried down five or six pages, they may not be absorbed as well. Everyone has a point at which information overwhelms the system. If you put the clues at the beginning, everyone will trip over them again and again. Eventually, one of their idiots will say, "Hey. Look at this, guys." Bingo. The raters will think they solved the mystery and deserve the Dick Tracy Award. It worked for me. Several others have deployed it to lethal effect. John Bisig (1958–2011) did this all by himself and netted 280 percent. He passed on Mother's Day last year and is our poster child for HCVets. He did it in fourteen months. He followed my Dave Del Dotto cash flow system to a T.

## How Many Claims Is Too Many?

Many Vets arrive with a laundry list of claims that runs into twenty or more items. This is a bad idea. This makes you look like someone who slips and falls down in supermarkets and files claims for a living. You want to be taken seriously. You want one claim to be the center of your contentions. Win that first and then come back with a list of secondary ailments caused by it. Vets who file numerous claims simultaneously have a very high loss rate. If there are two distinct medical conditions in play such as hepatitis and a back disorder, that would be acceptable. When VA raters see a long list of claims, they mentally deny many without beginning the process of looking at the facts. You want an open-minded individual with no agenda looking at this. Their habit is to deny anyway, so don't give them any additional ammunition.

The object of following this plan of attack is to win your claim at the regional level and avoid a long wait for the appeal process to make its way through the courts. Assembling all the data in advance allows you to see what VA has too. You will need your service medical records anyway in order to create a nexus letter. Your doctor cannot in good conscience write it without being able to see your whole medical history. Additionally, VA is in the habit of saying their doctor's nexus is more informed than yours because he saw *all* the medrecs. Most Vets who come to me late in the process are forced to play catch-up and assemble all this after they have been denied. This almost always causes a delay of three or four years and guarantees an appeal. Winning locally is the ticket as it usually can be done in less than sixteen months. Once the claim goes to DC, it can be remanded numerous times for more information. This is required because most regional offices are sloppy and do not perform the proper paperwork before it's sent to DC. The most common remand is for SSI records. VA knows this and yet they send it off to DC without it. When the VLJ sees this, he sends it back to be corrected and readjudicated. That will cost you fifteen months at a minimum each time. It is not unheard of for a Vet to consume ten years at this with an out-to-lunch VSO. Hell, your representative doesn't care how long it takes. It's not their claim! This creates employment for him. Time is of the essence to you because, in most cases, your illness has incapacitated you to the point of financial ruin. VSOs do not share your concerns. They have all the time in the world. VA has a similar mind-set.

When filing, an aggressive stance is not advised. Biting the hand that is about to feed you is bad form. Take a cheerful or neutral position. I'm sure you are angry for the way VA has treated you, or will be soon, but you must set that aside. You are going to come into contact with many personnel involved in this. Each one is going to study your demeanor, dress, personal appearance, and how you carry yourself. You certainly want to seem professional. You seek something for which you are legitimately entitled. There's no need to beg and plead for it. On the other hand, a nasty, insulting position will simply piss them off.

Think of your claim as a recipe. You are preparing to bake something, so you need to make sure you have all the ingredients on hand before starting. You cannot compromise and use baking powder in place of baking soda. Cutting any corners in this process will not yield the results you anticipate and desire. Never make the mistake of thinking you are smarter than the VA. They've been doing this since the War of 1812 and have it down to a fine art. Some of us—very many, I might add—have stubbed our toes learning it. I have had more than twenty Vets follow this religiously and win in less than fifteen months. They are amazed that it isn't *more* difficult.

## Tell the Truth at All Times

A few cautions are in order. Never lie or stretch the truth. VA has all your records. If you flunked a piss test for opiates in 1973, they remember. They can and often will do a criminal background check (CBI) on you if you have any drug/alcohol history. It costs me $39.95 to sign up for a year, and I'm sure VA gets a fleet rate. There are many (including all VSOs) who will contend that this is absurd. VA regularly comes up with information such as time served in a prison that they can only have obtained from a CBI. Assuming you may have some negative history, cheerfully address it as minor and make light of it. Being guilty of using drugs once or twice can be overcome. Repeated use leading to disciplinary action or chemical rehabilitation is far more of a hurdle but is still not insurmountable. Lying or failing to admit it implies deceit and will destroy your credibility as a witness. You don't want that in the claim. Once your credibility is compromised, all of it is. Lay evidence presented that *is* true will be thrown out like a baby with the bathwater. I really want all of you to understand this. VA gives your lay testimony great probative value. You are considered an excellent witness in your own defense unless, and until, you or the evidence proves otherwise. Often, this can be a make-or-break point in a claim. Preserving this credibility, for Veterans, is paramount. Anything you testify to under oath is considered to be the unvarnished truth, unless it is inherently incredible. You cannot diagnose yourself medically unless you are an RN or a doctor. Combat medics are accorded some leeway on this.

## Using Care with Witnesses

Having a witness provide testimony on your behalf is just as important as your own testimony. Counseling them like a defense attorney is all well and fine. If they are going to provide live testimony before a VLJ, be careful. I suggest a written notarized affidavit rather than a live appearance. You can control the content and prevent an undesirable comment from becoming a stain on the record. I suggest the notarization because, while it is not needed, it adds certain legitimacy to the statement.

## Consider a Hearing

**What you will need:** Submit a request for a RO hearing after denial. Time limit is one year from denial. Request can be filed on Form 21-4138 or regular 8.5 x 11 stationery.

If you are the nervous sort or not inclined toward public speaking, a Board or RO hearing can be scary. I prefer the live version to the videoconference one because it allows a VLJ to see how serious you are. They are excellent judges of character. They do this for a living. Someone trying to game the system does not have the same style and will appear dull and conniving. Their heart isn't in it because they are not genuine. Look the judge or hearing officer in the eye constantly and show strength. The eye contact allows them to see your face and your intensity. Looking down or away from the judge is a sign of dishonesty.

There are two varieties of this. The first one is the RO hearing. This is in conjunction with a decision review after denial. If, and only if, you have some really good evidence to rebut your denial, ask for the RO hearing.

The BVA hearing is after any other denials and you ask for it on your Form 9 substantive appeal.

## Know Your Time Limits

You have more than one shot at this unless you step on your necktie and miss a deadline. I have done this. You lose everything you have assembled. When you start over, you have to arrive with new and material evidence to add to all that you have provided in the prior claim.

It's far easier to be denied, then return within the allotted time and add to the existing record. This continues the same claim stream for as long as you keep it current and viable. I have seen claims that festered for over a decade because of repeated remands from the BVA or the court.

## The Squeaky Wheel

The truth is that you can wear them down with time. You won't find this written anywhere. An actively prosecuted claim with new evidence that helps to shed light on the case will eventually carry the day. VA will tire of this and eventually concede that you have made your case. They are inundated with millions of Veterans every year. When yours continues to fester like an open wound, someone will eventually want to clear off the desk and move on. This is when you will truly be given the benefit of the doubt. If your claim is appealed up to the BVA and they remand it for stupidity, again the chances you will prevail increase tenfold. If it's remanded by the CAVC to the RO, chances are you have won already. Assuming you had something to hang your hat on in the beginning, VA will be more likely to grant it. They have so many fish to fry that they don't worry about the occasional one who gets away. This may be your saving grace, but you will never know if you fail to appeal and allow the claim to lapse. Often it is no more than a piece of paper and a brief "I wish to appeal because the following was done wrong . . ." If 60 percent of these return from the CAVC on a remand, you would be foolish to overlook the odds.

## What Are My Odds of winning?

Presently, over 1 million Vets file claims every year. Roughly 15 percent are approved. That's approximately 150,000 Veterans. Of those 850,000 denied, only fifty thousand are appealed to the Board of Veterans Appeals. That is 5.9 percent—a very small number. Of the fifty thousand appealed to the BVA, approximately 22 percent are eventually granted. That's a whopping eleven thousand Veterans. Of those fifty thousand claims appealed to the BVA, approximately 4,500 go on to the Court of Appeals for Veterans Claims (CAVC) for appeal. Okay, this is where it gets interesting. Of the 4,500 claims that are appealed up to the CAVC, 2,700—or 60 percent—are either overturned for a win or remanded for errors. This shows your odds of winning continue to increase when appealed. In the end, your chance of winning a contested appeal is more like 30 percent. This book will show you how to increase it far higher. The weeding out process is calculated to make you give up. Some give up and others settle for far less than their due. VA has a habit of lowballing you on your rating too. This may take an appeal to fix in some cases. In fact, many claims are granted at 0 percent compensation. VA will tell you that this allows you to use the VA medical system. Not. It allows you to use it for your service-connected injury only. You have to pay for the rest. If you're broke and homeless, they won't charge you. That is the only exception to the rule.

## B
## Beginning the Claim—Basics

For your entertainment throughout this process, you can log on to VA's new site, Ebenefits, and follow the progress of your claim (https://www.ebenefits.va.gov/ebenefits-portal/ebenefits.portal).

There are a few things you have to do to sign up. It's like watching paint dry. The claim will move forward one American Idol season at a time. You will see it move by leaps and bounds over a two-year process culminating in a conclusion. If you lose, you can follow the progress at the BVA in equally slow motion for several more years. Actually, learning how to bowl may be more exciting.

## Three Types of Claims

There are, in my mind, three distinct and different claims that vary slightly in their prosecution. I divide them into (1) regular claims for disease/injury, (2) hepatitis C claims, and (3) PTSD claims. They are all done similarly but require slightly different treatment to win. Normal claims will almost always require evidence in your SMRs of an injury in service and a continuing history since (called chronicity). HCV and claims similar to it will require a unique nexus letter that sometimes depends heavily on a doctor willing to say (speculate) that you contracted it thirty years or more ago. These claims are difficult because there may be no evidence of any hepatitis in your SMRs. PTSD claims require you to have a stressor or seminal moment in combat you can point to. A sexual assault PTSD claim is very similar, and VA has recently lowered the bar for these claims. However, they now insist their (VA) doctors do the nexus exams and diagnose it.

## Preexisting Symptoms
## 38 CFR §3.303(c)

Some of you will have evidence in your SMRs of preexisting symptoms. This is not always a drawback to service connection. If this was noted on entry, any manifestation of it later in service will be assumed to be the same thing. In order to be service connected, you need to prove that your service made the prior injury worse. You can also say the injury simply became worse during your service. Your nexus doctor will have to state that the injury underwent an increase in severity because of your service. Again, you will have to show the continuity of chronicity through to the present. Below is the VA's regulation on this.

## 38 CFR §3.303(c)

**(c) Preservice disabilities noted in service.** There are medical principles so universally recognized as to constitute fact (clear and unmistakable proof), and **when** in accordance with these principles **existence of a disability prior to service is established,** no additional or confirmatory evidence is necessary. Consequently with notation or discovery during service of such residual conditions (scars; fibrosis of the lungs; atrophies following disease of the central or peripheral nervous system; healed fractures; absent, displaced or resected parts of organs; supernumerary parts; congenital malformations or hemorrhoidal tags or tabs, etc.) with no evidence of the pertinent antecedent active disease or injury during service **the conclusion must be that they preexisted service.** Similarly, **manifestation of** lesions or **symptoms of chronic disease from date of enlistment**, or so close thereto that the disease could not have originated in so short a **period will establish preservice existence thereof.** Conditions of an infectious nature are to be considered with regard to the circumstances of the infection and if manifested in less than the respective incubation periods after reporting for duty, they will be held to have preexisted service. In the field of mental disorders, **personality**

**disorders which are characterized by developmental defects or pathological trends in the personality structure manifested by a lifelong pattern of action or behavior, chronic psychoneurosis of long duration or other psychiatric symptomatology shown to have existed prior to service with the same manifestations during service, which were the basis of the service diagnosis, will be accepted as showing preservice origin. Congenital or developmental defects, refractive error of the eye, *personality disorders* and mental deficiency as such are *not diseases or injuries* within the meaning of applicable legislation.** (emphasis mine)

### 38 CFR §3.306

**(a) General.** A preexisting injury or disease will be considered to have been aggravated by active military, naval, or air service, where there is an increase in disability during such service, unless there is a specific finding that the increase in disability is due to the natural progress of the disease.

VA adheres to the idea that anything noted at entrance, unless proven otherwise, is not service connected. I mentioned earlier that they have built a nice escape hatch into "personality disorders" (PDs). Many Vets from all wars have come home with mental disorders now characterized and recognized as PTSD. The military has a handshake agreement with itself (the VA) to nod, wink, and call it PD. This can include antisocial personality, passive aggressive tendencies, obsessive compulsive disorder, etc. That was the crux of the matter at Joint Base Lewis McChord's Madigan Hospital in March 2012. Soldiers with legitimate PTSD were being downrated to minor personality disorders to save the VA money from what we can gather. Why else would they do this?

## The Mirror Test

The next step is a moral one. I would ask every one of you to stand in front of a mirror and look yourself in the eye. Are you doing this because you have a legitimate claim, or is this simply a ploy to obtain benefits fraudulently? You must be prepared for this to come back and bite you if it isn't above board. VA can and will prosecute you and put you behind bars if you try to cheat. You served America. She owes you if you were injured on the job and it's chronic. If you suddenly develop diabetes type 2 at sixty-six years of age and you weigh 380 pounds, chances are you got it from a poor diet. Don't blame it on Agent Orange. I know you *can* do that if you were in Vietnam, but should you? It's a moral dilemma only you can answer. VA may fight you tooth and nail over it, and then again, they probably won't. It's $251/month maximum, which is nothing. If you feel you were hosed and want to go after them over it, do so. If you were never anywhere near where it was sprayed, I think you should reconsider. You, alone, must live with your choice. The same applies to diseases. If you became a raging drug addict during or after service and became infected with HIV/HCV, the risk was the drugs, not the tattoo you got in Da Nang at 0400 hours in 1968 when you were toasted. Again, the mirror test is advised. VA may grant your claim, but then again, they may not.

## 38 CFR §20.900(c)
## Rule "900"

This is not widely known until you get to the BVA in DC, but any Vet who is suffering a life-threatening illness or can prove financial hardship can have his or her claim advanced on the docket. This can be a lifesaver for some considering how long it takes. You must ask for it. Do this when you file the claim. You will be required to prove it either by your medical records or by proof of major debt. These guys are assholes, but everyone has a heart in their shoe. If you are given this, it will mean everything goes much faster. What usually might take fifteen months may get done in eight to ten months. If it's a simple claim for increase, it can be done in two or three.

## How to Phrase the Claim

Many Vets phrase their claims incorrectly. They leave out something important or include way too much information. For instance, if you are going to claim hepatitis C, you may want to be more generic and leave it at hepatitis period. There are five alphabetical flavors of hepatitis now and three medically recognized flavors that are self-induced or caused by medications. What if you claim C, and it turns out to be chronic B or worse--autoimmune hepatitis? VA has been known to politely deny you because you *don't* have it. They are supposed to consider all possibilities, but then again, they are also supposed to accord you the benefit of the doubt. You are not a doctor. You have no medical training. Why would you want to venture a guess on this? Be absolutely certain of what you have and then file for it with a simple "liver disorder." Let them sort it out, but make sure you have the high ground with it. This way, when they deny, you can submit new evidence to prove it and keep your original filing date. Extra nexus letters are excellent backup too

## Filing Language

You are going to choose a disease/injury that happened to you while serving. You are not a doctor and cannot diagnose yourself. Do not try to do so. Phrase you request as "Entitlement to service connection for…" As

I mentioned earlier, if you have secondary illnesses related to the main one you are filing for, I suggest winning the primary one first. You are going to collect this compensation payment for life. Some are greedy and want to get on the gravy train for everything now. I personally think this is a bad idea. As I mentioned, claimants with a laundry list of twenty or thirty items generally get their denial with little or no serious research on VA's part. A claim for lower back pain and perhaps diabetes 2 (with Vietnam service) will stand a good chance of winning if supported by medrecs and a nexus. A follow on claim for radiculopathy into one or both legs after winning also stands a better chance because VA now considers your lay testimony to be a credible. You may lose a thousand dollars by waiting to win before filing, but what the heck? File 10 claims that are dubious and lose them all or focus on the one causing you to be disabled and win it? It's a decision you can choose to ignore if you feel very, very confident. Statistics on mega filings are not in your favor. I saw one while doing research that contained eighty-five different claims. Result? VA 85, Vet 0.

Some who have filed have read through part 4 of 38 CFR and are aware of exactly what is required to attain a specific ratings percentage (http://www.law.cornell.edu/cfr/text/38/4).

This will be discussed in another chapter, but it isn't impermissible to request a specific rating percent based on your degree of disability with your entitlement request. Thus "Entitlement to service connection and a rating of 20 percent for diabetes type II" is acceptable. I wouldn't be quite so specific on back claims or PTSD so as to not appear *too* knowledgeable. Remember, you're not a doctor. The same can be said for hepatitis. There are numerous types (A, B, C, D, F), and some which are not transmitted (steatohepatitis and autoimmune hepatitis). Based on that, I would keep it simple. Ask for hepatitis or liver disorder—period. Don't be specific. Let the VA doctors sort it out. When I came down with it in 1971, I thought it was the infectious food-borne variety (A). It turned out to be viral (B and C). When I filed in 1994, I claimed hepatitis B because that's what my dermatologist found. I didn't find out about C for another year. I filed in 2007 (like a dunce) for C. Its conceivable VA may dither and say you filed for B, but it's C or vice versa. I'm surprised they *didn't* treat me this way. The law says they have to develop all the possible theories on how you got it, but they don't always do that. What is certain is that VA will try to say the HCV you have now isn't the HAV or HBV you had in 1971.

If you can see or feel your injury symptoms, you can discuss them legally. Anything that comes to you via your five senses (hearing, touch, taste, sight and smell) is within your realm of testimony. Claiming that you got hepatitis from a pneumatic air injection vaccination device must be stated by a medical professional. You cannot say this. The reason is that a medical conclusion is beyond your realm of knowledge. Similarly, you should file for PTSD as a "mental disability—not otherwise specified (NOS)." You must choose your disease generically to protect yourself. You can at a later time on appeal say you're not a doctor and simply filed for what you thought was right. VA will *try* to interpret what it is you're filing for and change it anyway, so it's no big deal at this stage. It is important to control this process by framing the claims language in the beginning as closely as possible to the disease/injury in service without being perfectly correct.

## Established Disease or Injury

You need a track record of having visited your doctor on a somewhat regular basis. Your disease/injury must be obvious. There cannot be any disagreement on whether it's one thing, multiple things, or still a sketchy diagnosis. You are trying to prove your injury is chronic—that is, it's a longstanding problem. It can't be something that just surfaced when you went skiing last weekend. If you suffered an injury in service and file your claim thirty or forty years later with no after-service treatment, it will fail. This is established law that cannot be overcome. It is true in *all* cases except PTSD and cryptogenic diseases like hepatitis C. There were no tests for hepatitis C prior to 1989. In fact, there was no commercially available test until 1992. This is a classic example of the need for documented risks or stressors and a strong nexus. The risks will have to have been while you were serving. If you broke your leg sky diving five years after serving, it is negative evidence against your claim for an injured leg in service. The risk or injury has to be while in service with no similar events in between. I have seen VA find evidence of an injury after service that the Vet didn't report and he lost.

Drug or alcohol abuse while in service that results in injury and/or disease is considered willful misconduct and will not be service connected. If you get lung cancer, you cannot claim for it now. If you fail to disclose willful misconduct and VA finds out *after* they grant service connection, you will lose your rating and be liable for repayment of any compensation already received. If VA feels you did this fraudulently, they may refer it to the U.S. attorney for prosecution rather than just ask for the money back. They have the option to prosecute you criminally as well. This can result in a jail sentence.

# C
## Collecting the Evidence

**Documents needed**: VA Form 10-5345, Release of Medical Records; VA Form 21-4142, Consent to Release Forms to VA: any pertinent medical records from your private doctors; service medical and military records; laboratory reports; X-rays; any records being held by a VAMC; buddy letters; letters from spouse, siblings, dependents, etc.

Collecting the evidence is quite possibly the easiest part of what you have enlisted to do here. You want to obtain this yourself. You can easily get it, and you can prescreen you records for things doctors write that would blow your socks off. Some doctors don't like us. If you smoke and the doctor tires of telling you to knock it off, he may enter something such as "Joe came in with another sinus infection and reeks of tobacco. May be using sinus issues to obtain pain medication. Borderline for drug-seeking behavior." Mind you, I am not suggesting taking this out of your medical records. I am suggesting you be prepared to deal with it. If it has nothing to do with your claim, I wouldn't submit it. A sinus infection would have no bearing on any claim except a claim for sinus problems.

Even were you to use a VSO, you would still do this. It might upset their idea of how to stack the applecart, but you will be glad you did. This gives you the tactical advantage to view anything that the VA may attempt to use as negative evidence against your claim. Allowing VA to obtain it and then having them lose it is also for consideration. They are good at it by now. In fact, their reputation for losing things rivals only their history of misbegotten justice.

We've already discussed obtaining the SMRs and military records, so we needn't go over that again.

That gives you three important files. If you're filing multiple major disease/injury claims, make duplicate copies of the pertinent medical records for each injury and make individual folders for each claim. Some medical records will have the information for both (or more) claims, and you will need a copy of the same page for each file.

# D
## Organizing the Evidence

If you have an office in your home or a spare bedroom, you can spread all this out in nice organized piles. If you are a type A personality and have a filing cabinet, it will take up less space. Regardless of which way you do it, the idea is to assemble it in a way that an *idiot* can follow. Keep in mind that is who is going to try to decipher it at the VA regional office. You will need to show all this to the medical person(s) you choose to provide the nexus letter(s). All your good intentions with color-tabbed folders and collated evidence by year and month will be hopelessly mixed up as soon as it hits the C-File. I did all the careful preparation I have seen other sites advocate. When they send your file out to do a C&P exam, it gets hamburgered. I present it in an orderly manner now, but I know better. You can pile it all into a paper bag in no particular order, and they'll still monkey with it. I've had Vets submit it all electronically on discs, and guess what? They download it all into paper format so that they can assemble it like a puzzle.

When I am finished organizing the evidence for filing, I lay each claim folder out and examine each for a complete timeline of the following:

a. evidence/information
b. pertinent SMRs from service
c. intercurrent (newer) private medical records
d. the nexus letter(s)
e. the proper wording for the claim.
f. statements from others

Again, I counsel Vets to be careful here. A claim with more than three major life-threatening diseases and a bunch of minor ones is like a tax return with too many deductions. The idea is to create a Corvette, not an eighteen-wheeler with forty feet of extra cargo behind it. VA often will grant one claim and defer others for development. If you are claiming a lot of secondary illnesses/diseases to one of your major ones, it follows that they can't grant the secondary ones until they determine the primary ones. With six secondaries, you bog the claim down. Worse, the rater gets so confused he can't concentrate. When that happens, it's easier to deny than do the hard work. Remember my earlier warning that it makes you look sleazy or like throwing spaghetti on the wall to see if any of it sticks. Another problem with secondary diseases is that you are working with a VA rater who is not knowledgeable in medicine. He doesn't know the difference between diabetes and diarrhea or which comes first. If you tack diabetes on as a secondary to hepatitis, the rater will try to figure out if diabetes is caused by Agent Orange even if you were never there (Vietnam). They are obligated to check to be sure. They will also search the medical records to see if you had it in service. All this is done before they even try to connect it via the nexus letter you sent in with it. This slows the claim down, which is what we're trying to avoid.

This book will counsel you to do many things differently than traditional how-to/DIY Vet sites and books. Sites are fine, but unless you have them open on five tabs to view different chapters, it can be confusing. A book lets you insert little bookmarks in and peel it open to what you want. Buy the color tabs at Office Depot and put them on the different pages if you want. Sometimes analog is better for doing this. Keep in mind that you can find a lot of this in more detail on my Web site: http://asknod.wordpress.com/ or asknod.org.

This will also give you more access to the legal decisions from the BVA and the CAVC/Fed, circuit that I used to discover all this.

You are going to obtain this compensation for life, and it will increase in severity. New illnesses associated with a disease and additional radiculopathy to a back/leg injury are a given. If this happens, you will be filing again for increases or actual new secondary claims. Absent any fraudulence on your part, this grant is for life. Why be greedy? The important goal is 100 percent disability if you are entitled to it. Being service connected for chronic myelogenous leukemia is far more important than being rated for hemorrhoids or tinnitus. Nobody ever died from them. Some Vets go at this ass backward. They slowly assemble a library of small wins on tinnitus, hemorrhoids, hammer toe, acne vulgaris, pes planus, and a scar or two. Each one of these will usually never amount to more than 10 percent. VA also doesn't add them up like 10 + 10 + 10 + 10 = 40. Four tens equal 34 percent, which rounds down like the IRS to 30 percent. It would take ten 10 percent ratings to reach a 70 percent disability. It would take fifteen 10 percent ratings to reach 80 percent. It would take twenty 10 percent ratings to attain 90 percent. Lastly, it would take twenty two to reach 100 percent. Chronic, ingrown toenails are not why this book was written, but the recipe on how to win is identical.

In summary, you want the most bang for the diseases you may die from. Injuries that make you bedridden or unable to take care of yourself or your family are it. You want to do it now. Delay allows the VA to slip in the argument that it cannot possibly be because of the parachuting injury in service. In the forty years after service, you had a lot of small injuries documented in your private medical records. You can't hide them. VA may still ask your private providers to cough up what they have on you. Get these important battles under your belt and then file for the secondaries as being an offshoot of the original injury. You will need a nexus for these too but can have your original nexus letter written to include them now. Then it's easier to point to them and say, "Look. Right there. I'm already good to go on that one." VA can do little but agree. This usually means they will just send you out for a C&P exam, and you'll be rated in several months.

Once you pass 100 percent, the next milestone is 60 percent for an increase of $331/month. That's actually a lot easier than it looks if you have HCV and a major back issue. Add in some secondaries from the hepatitis, sprinkle in tinnitus, and DM2; and you're there. I don't advocate cheating, but these are things you can do (if you know about them) to improve the paycheck. Face it; you're not going to retire in Hawaii on this. Even with SSD/SSI, you may only net $4,500 a month. It's tax-free, but gas is $5 per gallon there, and milk is even more. An amount of $331 more a month might not sound like the cat's pajamas, but it's $3,972 more a year. By anybody's reckoning, you will be on borderline poverty, so don't feel like you're cheating. You are the one who chose to risk your life, and you are now bearing the consequences of that decision by losing your ability to earn money. What you get back is chump change compared with what you could make if you were healthy. Don't lose sight of that.

# E
# The Meat of the Claim
# Your Nexus Letter(s)

Consider visiting my website and reading about nexus letters in great detail including an example at http://asknod.files.wordpress.com/2012/05/nexus-bible.pdf

The MD, PA, or ARNP will need to see your medical records from service as well as the ones post service. Importantly, they must state that they did so. In addition, they will need to defend why they think that your disease or injury is more likely to have occurred in service rather than before or after. They must point to a reason. You can help by researching this. Assembling articles that support your theory (if necessary) is important. This will give the doctor more ammunition. In the case of using pneumatic vaccination devices (jetguns) as a risk for HCV, VA will say that it is plausible but unproven. The reason for this is that VA has never commissioned a study to find out. I personally do not think they *want* to know. Were it proved to be the culprit it would break the piggybank. If your doctor feels this is the disease vector and states his reasons clearly and concisely, you will win. It all boils down to this one letter and how well it is written. I have reams of evidence in favor of this theory on my web site, and Vets have used it to win.

When filing for HCV, you need to write your own summary of why you think the risk you claim is the one that caused it. If there are multiple risks, we suggest including them *all* at the beginning. The reason is to appear credible. If VA denies based on the risks you listed, and you arrive with a brand new batch while the claim is still in progress, it will appear you are grasping at straws to win.

If your claim is for an injury such as a back disorder, the evidence is going to have to appear somewhere in the SMRs. If it is an aggravation of an injury before service, the same is still true. There simply has to be a noting of an injury or traumatic event that precipitated the current malady. VA will focus on anything *after* service as the reason for this. They will also try to say it was acute and resolved before discharge. That's their job. You have to be persistent and stay focused on everything you say about this. There can be no "I think it was …" statements pro or con. It happened one way, and that's what happened. The C&P doctor might say, "Gee, buddy, do you think you might have injured it after service doing construction?" If you say something neutral like "I don't know. Maybe," your case is done. That will turn into "The claimant stated that he injured his back doing construction work sometime after service. He feels this is the reason for his lower back etiology." I hear all of you laughing at this. It happens so frequently that it is painful to talk about.

When you entered service, they examined you from top to bottom and listed all tattoos and scars on item #39 on the SF 88 entrance physical. They even noted the smallpox scar. They like to make themselves immune to claims after service, and this is the way to do it. If they don't detect it at the entry physical and it isn't documented in private records prior to service, you are presumed to be of sound body and mind unless otherwise noted. This is known as the presumption of soundness and is an important concept. It works in your favor if you have a documented injury. It represents the proof that you didn't have it when you entered. If you did, this becomes the baseline for the injury. They can always use the first measurement to go off if it got worse. The system has been around since the Civil War.

When you left service, they didn't always do this. Many were given their walking papers without an exam. Some guys I talked to said they could sign off on a form to skip it. If this happened to you, you can submit a buddy statement from a friend or loved one. Have them swear to your arrival home with an injury or tattoo. They cannot diagnose what you had, but they can sure describe what they saw. If you winced in pain standing up or sitting, they can say that. Have their statements notarized.

Some of you may have had an STD or non-gonococcal urethritis in service. This too is a risk for HCV, but you must have your doctor say these things in the letter. If it happened, it's in the records. If you claim multiple risks, the order of highest probability must be assigned to the highest risk. A smaller percentage of risk would be given to the lesser risks. Thus, it would be permissible for the good doctor to say it is "more likely than less likely" that the biggest risk was the tattoo received in service. He can then say that it is "at least as likely as not" that the STDs were the cause. He could also say that in his medical opinion, the jet gun was the risk factor most likely to have been the culprit, and the reasoning is that they are inherently unsanitary and their use has been discontinued by the military. There are many risks to choose from. Whichever you choose, your doctor must defend it with logic and scientific theses. A bald claim, absent any supporting medical records, is not considered evidence. With evidence in the medrecs, it is easier for the doctor to connect it. Obviously if you had documented hepatitis in your SMRs in 1967, it could be said that was "most likely" the time of inception. Again, if the doctor says it, it's gold. Having more than one nexus letter is not a requirement but is great insurance.

## Multiple Nexus Letters

Whenever possible, I suggest that Vets arrive with two nexus letters. This puts VA at a strategic disadvantage. You have not one but two doctors willing to stand behind you. VA will have to obtain at least two of their own to balance this or prove that yours are suspect for some reason. They are not inclined to do this, and they will usually fold if your letters are constructed as I have described. Arriving with only one may tempt them to meet you head on and fight. If you lose and appeal, they may choose to seek an independent medical opinion (IMO). Three guesses who supplies that "independent" assessment. You do not want to find yourself in this poker game. You always want to hold the high ground and defend it. The principle of a well-planned claim is an offensive one. There is no room for retreat and regrouping. VA will sense any weakness and leap on it. If your doctor has tried to connect an injury in service to something really far-fetched, VA will go for their own IMO.

VAMC doctors are actually allowed to write nexus letters, but some may refuse to. They changed the law back at the turn of the century. They are not obligated to, certainly, but if they know the circumstances and are comfortable with you, they will. You can write the whole thing out for their signature only as an example. You can and should hand them an outline with the dos and don'ts listed. Most doctors are very strong-willed and insist on writing their own. These usually won't pass the test because the language is too iffy. The use of the words "could have, might have, probably, possibly, conceivably, believable" and "rule out" are ones that do not work. Unfortunately, doctors love those choices. The VA has its own unique way of doing this. Their unequivocal method is to couch it in the following quantitative terms:

> The evidence is in equipoise (50–50)
> At least as likely as not (above 50 percent)
> More likely than less likely (above 50 percent)
> Most likely (above 50 percent)
> Is due to (100 percent)

Every doctor is an island in this regard. Let them have their way with the phrases, but they have to keep the actual nexus worded in these narrow confines. Without it, the nexus is not useful. VA often provides their VA examiner's opinion. Oddly, all he can do is cite to a doctor. He is not allowed to opine even though many do. If this happens, you can throw theirs out the window and say yours is by a recognized medical professional. By the same token, if you provide none, they may provide one written by whomever they choose. They have been known to be lazy and deny based on your failure to provide any nexus at all. Be careful. More Vets lose at this initial stage because they entered the arena thinking VA would look at their evidence and grant based on what they presented. VA will look at it and always deny now without a nexus. They have to. You must present evidence that proves your case. The doctor supplies the missing link. Unless there is concrete proof in your medrecs, you have to have this. I had medrecs saying I had hepatitis in service *and* a nexus all to no avail. VA's IMO doctor still had to look at it too. The VA is extremely anal about all of this. I cannot emphasize how important this part is. It's the make-break item every time.

As for getting a letter from a VA doctor (or any doctor), go slowly. Try to get your PCP (personal care physician) to think about all the different causes. See him on a regular basis, so he remembers you. Try to ask him questions about the disease/injury even if you know the answers. This will tell you what he thinks about you and your specific illness. If you ask about the possibility of picking up hepatitis from a jet gun and he blows coffee through his nose laughing, it's safe to say he's not a candidate for your letter. It usually is best to ask for a specialist in your problem area. A gastroenterologist is going to have a better idea of what is or isn't a hepatitis risk than a general practitioner or ARNP. By sounding these doctors out innocently, you can always figure out whether they may help. Try to act dumb. Doctors hate Internet wannabe doctors like us. My favorite is to go into it from the negative side: "Gee, Doc, I read that AO causes DM2. Is that a crock of shit or what?" Nine times out of ten, Dr. Doright will chime in with an "Oh, no. It's true." This tells you a lot about the guy. You can build on that. This is what Vets have shared with me. They said the VA doctors get frightened easily. They don't want to be seen as the enemy by the VA. That's who writes their paycheck. When they get comfortable with their job and see how the VA screws Vets, they change. Some will never do it even if you ghost write it for them.

There is a mounting body of evidence that VA has told its doctors to quit writing nexus letters. I have had several friends who tell me the VA's doctors say they are forbidden to. The regulations say they can, but if the unwritten law says they'll get dinged for it, then that is what will happen. I'm sorry. I can't fix that one for you. There are different outfits that will, but they charge an arm and a leg with no guarantees.

Here is the latest I was able to derive from VA VHA regulations: http://www.nvlsp.org/images/VHADirective2007.pdf.

(1) Determination of causality and degrees of service connection for VA benefits is exclusively a function of the Veterans Benefits Administration (VBA). VHA providers often do not have access to military medical records, and may not be familiar with all the health issues specific to military service, such as environmental exposure. As a result, they may not feel comfortable in stating causality of a current condition. However, this does not preclude VHA providers from recording any observations on the current medical status of the veteran found in the medical record, including their current functional status. All pertinent medical records must be available for review by VBA.
**NOTE:** *VHA continues to provide compensation and pension*

(C&P) examinations and reports as requested by VBA, as part of any new disability claims or review process.

(2) Requests by a veteran for assistance in completing a VA disability claim are to be referred to VBA through official channels, but the clinician, if requested by the veteran, must place a descriptive statement in the veteran's medical record regarding the current status of the veteran's existing medical condition, disease, or injury, including prognosis and degree of function. This may then be requested by VBA for the purposes of making a claim determination

I discovered one thing by researching VA decisions and CAVC cases. VA can use a podiatrist to opine about HCV. They can use an ear, nose, and throat doctor to write your nexus for your back. They are allowed to do this and not even mention it. Lord help you if you try this. They'll gut you like a fish. If you are doing a private nexus (except for PTSD), it's best to use a specialist in the field. If denied, ask for the particulars on the doctor who made your decision. This is when they may let slip he's an obstetrician.

Many Veterans mistakenly believe that the C&P doctor is the one who makes the call on the service connection. Wrong. All he/she does is take your vitals and examine what you are claiming. They record the evidence and submit it to the VA. The VA examiner (the rater) then looks at everything in the file. He asks a PA, ARNP, or MD employed by the VARO to make the call. That is the medical nexus the VA depends on. They are only required to say why they are denying it. They may give a medical analysis of why, but it will list everything negative and nothing positive.

As of January 2012, the VA has a new policy on nexus letters for PTSD. The VA policy is that their doctors will now do the diagnosis and confirm the relationship to service. It may be that this will be declared illegal, but it appears to be law now (2012). Therefore, private nexus letters will not be accepted. If you have private medical records, I would still submit them if they help prove your case. VA has to look at them. What importance they attach to them will be their decision.

# F
# Overwhelming Evidence in SMRs that Precludes Need for Nexus

If there is a noted injury/disease in service in your SMRs, the VA will usually grant a claim. The evidence must show the same chronic condition exists today. Private medical records showing treatment after service are also needed. This is the only exception where a nexus letter isn't required.

VA is fond of reminding us we are not doctors. This permits them to say we cannot make weighty decisions about what caused our disease. This is odd because you are allowed to choose what you want to when you file the claim. If you're wrong on your own medical diagnosis, they love to point out your error. They allow it that far. You may testify to anything you want as long as it involves the five senses of sight, smell, hearing, taste, and touch. Thus you can testify that it was monsoon season when your skin turned yellow or right after the IED that your arm started bending in a different direction and hurt. Beyond that, it requires a doctor's pronouncement to identify any disease/injury.

If you had an injury or hepatitis in service, VA is always going to say it isn't the same as what you are suffering now. You must seal up that loophole with every conceivable thing the doctor can muster to write down. A strong statement that cuts off that line of thinking should be an important part of any letter.

You are obligated to supply VA with medical records that are pertinent. They must pertain to the injury or disease you are claiming. The law does *not* say you have to provide them with dental records to prove your back injury. Similarly, you do not need to provide X-rays of a broken arm for a hepatitis filing. VA will ask you to sign releases (VA 10-5345) for them to obtain all private records that you identify. The key phrase is "that you identify." Keep that in mind. I do not advocate dishonesty despite the fact that the agency you are preparing to do battle with engages in this practice. I simply mention it. Filing for a back injury in my mind does not involve the brain, so I read that as meaning they have no business looking into your psychiatric records. They will probably want to.

Once you assemble all the components, you should proceed to filing. Keep a copy of everything because they will inevitably call up and complain that you didn't supply them with it. In my case, they claimed they lost almost all of my private medical records. I drove them to Seattle personally to make sure they were there for the final adjudication. When I got a copy of my C-file in 2009, I was surprised to find two copies of them. They had them all along. Go figure. That's the kind of incompetence you'll be dealing with.

I would avoid doing the yellow highlighter pen on the records. These people are country bumpkins when it comes to deciphering the stuff. Don't confuse them. You can lead them to the watering hole, but you can't highlight the water. They will insist on doing the Sherlock Holmes imitation themselves. In fact, any attempt to point them to the true facts may backfire. They may feel that you are trying to railroad them. Vets have told me they were forced to do this after denial, so it may be better to employ it then.

# G
# Proceed to Go!
# Push Print

You now have hopefully assembled a pile of files. It now should consist of a VA Form 21-526, which you have downloaded. This will be the only

VA form you are obligated to fill out. I feel it's optional, but VA may go NASDAQ and screw it up. Take that potential out of their hands and make this minor concession. Any lay testimony you or your spouse, friend, buddy, or parent submits on your behalf must have this written at the bottom of the testimony:

"I certify that the statement above is true and correct to best of my knowledge and belief." Print your name below it, then sign and date it.

This is the same as putting your left hand on the Bible and holding your right hand up, saying, "I solemnly swear to tell the truth, the whole truth, and nothing but the truth, so help me, God." If you don't do this, they will put this in the "useless" pile.

I did have a Vet friend who filed his NOD on a paper towel. He was in a VAMC and was upset with the way he was being treated. He felt they might take him more seriously, and it worked. He mailed one to Senator (Name redacted) on the same stationery. They sent a representative over to talk to him and made sure he was happy. This is almost unheard of.

In addition to the 526, you should have any and all supporting Internet documents or studies that support your claims. You should have a current diagnosis for your illness and an iron-clad nexus or two with no holes in it. You have assembled all private medical records you feel will prove your treatment of this disease over the past years following your military service. You are not obligated to send your SMRs. Some VSOs will tell you not to. I would. VA is going to contact St. Louis and obtain all that, but it doesn't hurt. Do make sure you include the page where it notes the injury or disease though. Here I will point out a time saver. If you live relatively close to the VARO, I would suggest you hand-carry this package in and submit it in person. If not, send them in from a U.S. post office and use a certified mail return receipt requested (green card). This is *very* important. VA can, has, and will deny they got it. If you have proof, this guarantees your filing date. Once they sign for it, they can't deny they got it.

VA has long held that if you mail something in and do not have proof of it, then it can be construed that you never mailed it and are lying. This is the theory of the Common Law Mailbox Rule. *If* you can prove you sent it, then it is presumed that you *did*. VA, on the other hand, operates on the Presumption of Regularity Rule. They need no proof that they mailed it, and the law says if they did, it's presumed you received it. If someone steals it out of your mailbox, tough luck. The only exception to the rule is if they mail it to the wrong address.

You want to do this once and you want to make sure VA gets it *all*. I choke with laughter when someone says, "I gave it to my VSO to file." When I gave things to my VSO in American Lake to file, he sent them to the VAMC in Seattle. They, in turn, were supposed to transfer it over to the VARO mail bag. From what happened, I know some got lost because I ended up refilling many things. VA has never lost anything I sent via the CM-RRR (green card) method. Some Vet's sites suggest you send in the claim and wait for a letter to arrive asking for the evidence. You can always write back and say, "Refer to USPS CM#1234567890 delivery, signed by Clyde Clodiddlehopper on 3 June 2006. It's all there." VA's mailroom logs *everything* in. They know you sent it. They might lose it or shred it accidentally, but they have to acknowledge you sent it. You can't know how important that can be later on. It happens enough for me to warn you.

You are now going to experience a delay, on average of sixteen months. You will receive notice that they have the claim, and it is being processed within three months. If they need anything else, they usually contact you either via phone or letter. Be prepared to read War and Peace while you wait. I always continue to work on my claims as they are being reviewed. I investigated VA law on the subject and the ratings procedures. You will have ample time to do this and get familiar with the process. Give them a good telephone number they can reach you at during the day. They don't call after five o'clock when you get home. If they call during the day, you will get a message. A word to the wise. You cannot just "call" the VA rater back. It may have a "restricted" number. The number you see on the phone dial may be a switchboard outgoing call number. VA, as a rule, does not have any way to be reached unless they specifically give you a number to call back to. Your only way is to use the 800-827-1000 number. We call this Dial-a-Prayer. The "technician" who answers will screw it up royally. Be careful.

If your claim holds water, they schedule you for a compensation and pension examination. They may anyway to deny you. Most times, they will deny if there is nothing submitted to prove the claim.

## 38 USC and 38 CFR

There are two different sets of laws on the subject of claims. 38 USC (United States Code) are the statutes incorporated into law by Congress that state the law. Chapter 38 CFR (Code of Federal Regulations) deals with the regulations written by the VA secretary that implement these laws. Imagine it like this. 38 USC is the Second Amendment, which allows us to keep and bear arms. 38 CFR implements this at the local level and describes some of the places where you can and cannot do this. When 38 CFR argues with 38 USC, the VA secretary is obligated to change it. This is what occurs at the CAVC on a fairly regular basis. VA engages in "mission creep" and likes to read more into a regulation than there is. Often this produces results that were never intended. The Court has to clear this up frequently because the VA keeps doing it again and again.

There is no need to quote CAVC precedent to the RO. In fact, it is useless. They work from the M21-A1 adjudication manual. It's built into their computers and tells them what to do because most are not smart enough to do logical thinking. Similarly, there is no need to quote BVA decisions to them. BVA stuff is not precedence. It is simply what a judge held in the case of another Vet who was somewhat similarly situated. It won't help and can hurt if you depend on it.

By the same token, if you quote 38 CFR to the VA rater, he'll look at you like you're speaking Greek. They speak M-21. At the end, they will translate it into 38 CFR, but not before.

Here the book must diverge in two different directions. If you win, proceed to chapter 5.

# CHAPTER 4

## THE DENIAL

### A
### The First Denial at the RO

**Things you will need**: File Notice of Disagreement using computer paper or VA form 21-4138. Submit any additional evidence or nexus you have assembled in the meantime after initial filing. Use Pertinent 38 CFRs to show error.

Before I begin, let me distinguish between the M21-A1 Adjudications manual, chapter 38, Code of Federal Regulations, and precedential cases from the CAVC. All three are different and deserve an explanation of their importance at each stage of your claim. Here, at the lowest level, you are dealing with ants running helter-skelter, picking up the pieces of the claim, and carrying it back to the nest. They don't reassemble a bug they cut up when they get there. Things get confused, and it's not perfect. They take your evidence and feed it into their M-21 Ouija board. Out pops a decision according to what they put in. Error almost always occurs. You might win sometimes, but they still screw up the facts. Even though the RO will quote or refer to 38 CFR, the fact is they relied on the M-21. If you argue with them, it falls on deaf ears. You have no way of translating this into M-21 computer language. Nobody does, including the VA raters apparently. A warm body would have to do it manually. Needless to say, using CAVC Court precedents to make your case will be like walking in and discussing it in Laotian or Vietnamese. When you file the Notice of Disagreement, you can try to quote 38 CFR to them on why they did it wrong or why they came to the wrong conclusion, but it is almost useless. They want facts. They need written, documented, legitimate evidence. Rules? They don't need no stinkin' rules. Working with RO personnel, regardless of how well-meaning they are, is like talking to your dog. They know you are talking but don't really understand you unless it's "Ball!" or "Go with?"

When you reach the Board of Veterans Appeal (BVA), they do everything by chapter 38, Code of Federal Regulations, buttressed by 38 USC. They also cite to the CAVC as well for guidance.

If VA produces a denial that states their "VA examiner" has opined that it "is less likely than more likely" that it is from service, I suggest you ask to talk to this person or have them call you. You can do this by calling the 800 number and requesting the courtesy of a call back. Find out why immediately. This means your nexus is in trouble. If everything is done right, this should not happen. If it does, deficient evidence is to blame. Ask to see the C&P exam results and the name of any doctor involved if you did not see one named. Most often they have overlooked something that is important to winning.

I have seen Vets denied for many wrong reasons. Some are violations of their own regulations. Some are because of misinterpretation of the facts and almost all are because of stupidity on VA's part. VA is fond of saying something is not in your SMRs. They may choose to call a back injury an "acute orthopedic misadventure." If it isn't mentioned again, you healed. Period.

There is no guarantee you will win straight away. In the event of a denial, a close examination of why they chose to do this will be necessary. If it is truly because of a *lack* of evidence, VA will sometimes try to characterize it as *negative* evidence. No dice. Your nexus letter(s) are your protection. The doctor has analyzed all the records in making his decision. If this simply is a pissing match between VA's and your doctor's qualifications, the claim should be approved. VA will always try to find something wrong in a nexus letter provided by you. If you leave a theory or risk unguarded, they will pounce on it. They'll say your doctor didn't address it and theirs did; therefore, their doctor's nexus is more probative. Always remember, in an ex parte proceeding, you submit all your evidence and wait. VA has ample opportunity to develop what they need to rebut your evidence after you file. You want to avoid going to DC if you can. Therefore, you have to look at every conceivable loophole. Play devil's advocate and think of all the "what-ifs" the VA will cook up. The English language is their most potent tool. Knowing their buzz words will go a long way toward immunizing your claim against failure.

### Negative Evidence or Absence of Evidence?

When analyzing a denial, be very careful to parse every sentence as a stand-alone statement. If there is an assessment that the records do not support a contention, question this. Is it a medical finding that wasn't "discovered" until 1989? VA often will say something to the effect that there is no evidence of an injury in service. There doesn't need to be an injury, *per se*. What is important is that you went to seek *medical attention* for the injury. If they were unable to diagnose an injury because of the lack of MRIs in 1970, that is *not* "negative evidence," which weighs against you. It is simply "absence of evidence." There is a major difference between the two when it comes time to weighing everything. It may be the item needed to tilt the scales in your favor. VA will often leave out this fact (lack of MRIs to substantiate). This is a timeless trick Veterans should be aware of. I see it used extensively in every HCV claim. The VA examiner will say that there is no evidence of any "liver dysfunction" in service. They will carefully say there is no mention of HCV in your 1970s SMRs. What *isn't* said is that HCV was not discovered until 1989, and there was no test commercially available to the medical community until 1992. The mere "noting" of a condition while in service has been held to constitute proof of symptoms. The court actually phrased it as, "Symptoms, not treatment, are the essence of continuity of a disability." This was the famous Wilson v. Derwinski decision of 1991.

Similarly, a Vet could have been discharged for personality disorders, when in reality he suffered from diagnosable mental illness. The military has been guilty of this for decades going back to the Vietnam Boundary Dispute. They tried to resurrect this recently in the Iraq/Afghanistan Wars, but it blew up in their faces. Calling PTSD a personality disorder to avoid paying compensation for it has been exposed now so there shouldn't be any more of those claims. I did read in the newspapers that they are going to get tougher on the doctors to make sure no one is faking it. This, too, is a VA trick. Blame the Veteran for scamming the system when caught.

Where hepatitis is involved, VA used to state that the hepatitis in service was type A or acute. Acute is the medical term for something temporary that resolved. They will argue that no testing was done, and their doctor will say he thinks it isn't the same. Polymerase Chain Reaction (PCR) testing now reveals the truth so that argument is worthless. If you spot it, rebut it immediately. This was a much used ploy to deny ten years ago. Now the mere proof of *any* hepatitis in service is evidence enough to get traction, especially if you have the nexus. Vietnam Veterans are 60 percent more likely to have HCV than any other similar age group or occupation. Veterans as a whole are 40 percent more likely to have it if they served between 1958 and 1992. This argument alone is pretty powerful.

You have to point this out. VA will admit to nothing. They will not help you prove your claim against them although they say otherwise.

Word use and placement are VA's strong point and must be examined carefully. Some phraseology is deficient and has grammatical errors. Don't focus on those misspellings and dangling participles. Go straight to the meat of your denial and see if they have made their case. I said earlier that you need to have a seamless tapestry with no flaws or lack of continuity. Look for a fact that proves them wrong. Is it guesswork on VA's part? Can it be rebutted by evidence you somehow forgot to submit or felt was a matter of record? VA often mangles the facts to arrive at a denial. They sometimes change or artfully rephrase what you filed for to make it appear that you do not, indeed, suffer from it. Take a filing such as "porphyria cutanea tarda, as a *residual* of hepatitis *and/or* exposure to herbicides (Agent Orange)." VA took that one and turned it into two separate claims: (1) residuals of hepatitis and (2) PCT because of herbicides. They denied the residuals of hepatitis based on no evidence presented and denied the PCT based on no proof of being in Vietnam. Game. Set. Match. Next? This is the much-employed "divide-and-conquer" strategy. Some claims hinge on one another. VA calls these "inextricably intertwined." VA knows this and uses the technique to carefully divorce the two such that one is unsupported and causes both to fail. Proper phraseology at filing can protect you on appeal. I cannot stress the importance of this enough. Each claim should have support. Where two claims are part of one disease or injury, be clear to say so. Use the term inextricably intertwined too.

If you provide a medical history to your doctor that is unsupported by the record, this is called "history" by VA. It is just that, an unsubstantiated record of what *you told* the doctor. If you are merely reciting "your version," you need proof. It is more believable if you told the doctor twenty years before the claim. One of VA's potent tricks is to run your civilian records down by saying you simply told the doctor something and he wrote it down exactly as you reported it. If this is evidence *in* your favor, it is useless in their book. Should this "history" contain a fair amount of negative evidence about drug usage, it will suddenly become valuable admissible medical information that proves the case against you and is pertinent. VA tries to have it both ways. Always examine your medical records with an eye toward VA finding some minor admission or an irrelevant diagnosis and expanding on it to show your illness is not service connected. Veterans are amazed when they get their denials back. The smallest item is the smoking gun against the claim sometimes.

A minor notation of pelvic inflammatory disease (PID) can be construed to show a predilection toward sexual promiscuity. Hell, women get them from lots of things. VA will have you believe this is specifically indicative of a wild and crazy lifestyle. Ladies, prepare for this in advance and address it by proving you did no such thing.

Alcohol usage will always be used against you. The noting of consumption of a beer or two in the evening after work will be magnified to "over half a case a week." I learned the hard way never to acknowledge that I drank anything to protect myself against this. Your private doctor may not even list this, but when you get to the VA, it becomes a witch hunt. Veterans simply don't believe this until it blows up in their faces.

I guess I don't even need to go into the evils associated with left-handed tobacco. When asked, say something like "I'm a Mormon" or "Our church doesn't believe in that kind of stuff." This is an indirect answer. You are avoiding the question by substituting a parallel answer. A medical person taking your intake history will infer it as a negative answer. Bill Clinton used this technique a lot. The admission of even one experience—even without inhaling it—is going to be recorded as "patient admits to a history of regular usage of marijuana." I'm sorry but that is what you can expect. If you do not partake, and haven't since New Year's Eve in 1995, why even open Pandora's Box and stare into it? In order for this to work, you have to be able to pass their urinalysis. They can and will test you once you come into their medical system. As a general rule, any time they ask for the piss test, they're looking for illicit drugs or excessive alcohol use. It's easy to see too. If you are on morphine for pain, make sure they know that. Many Vets get a denial after fifteen months, and it says, "Claimant testified he didn't use drugs. Testing, however, revealed the presence of opiates. The VA examiner therefore feels the claimant is not a credible witness."

There is further case law (Federal Rules of Evidence or FRE) that says a patient is more likely than not to report the truth to a doctor because he has a vested interest in getting well and it aids in properly diagnosing his illness. While VA does not abide by the FRE on paper, they tend to incorporate the premise. This is true up to the point where the claim commences. After that, any statement to a doctor can be construed as an attempt to pad the record. I mentioned protecting your credibility earlier. This applies in spades here. Anything in your medical records, private or in service, must agree with all your testimony. Any variation will be pounced on to impeach your good word. This is why it is so important to construct your claim from the ground up and make sure all the pieces fit.

## Continuity

I don't know if any of you have ever visited a movie set. There is a group of people labeled "Continuity." Their assigned task is to keep everything in place from one shooting of a scene to the next. Every fork on a table must stay put, so they don't jump around or disappear if the scene has to be reshot. Likewise, your claim must have continuity. A timeline must be constructed and verified for accuracy. It wouldn't do to say you started to come down with this when you felt puke sick and reported to sick call in June 1978. What if the service medrecs show you went in for it in February 1979? VA will imply that your memory can't be trusted back that far and will cite this as evidence of it. They usually do it the tricky way and say, "The records are silent for any entries in June 1978." What they never say is that it shows up as February 1979. This is how they work. I'm serious. You will lose, and it will take a very long time, if ever, to fix it. Most Vets shrug and give up. They are not expecting it. Would you?

Continuity applies to the whole shooting match. Doctor's names, places, dates, and more will be tested for a seamless tapestry of uniformity that agrees with your version. Complete this ahead of time. Construct the timeline on paper in a synopsis form. The more you recall it, the more you will be able to "relive" it and remember even more.

This may not be the most important thing you do in life, but it will have enormous financial rewards sooner if it is done by the numbers. You will start having dreams about this era of your life. Keep a notebook handy to write down a friend's name that comes back to you or a place. Lucid moments are often like waking up from a dream. You will remember them briefly, so write them down before you lose them again.

To give you an example, I couldn't remember the name of my pilot I was flying with when I was wounded. It was forty years ago. I could remember his first name—Chuck—but his last name escaped me. The harder I tried to recall it, the more it eluded me. One day I was driving up Meadowlark Street and turned left onto ENGLEwood Avenue, and there it was! Chuck Engle, First Lieutenant USAFR. Unfortunately, he was dead and unavailable to testify, but it was important evidence in the claim. Put your brain in neutral and let it idle. Your subconscious mind will retrieve it and post it on the desktop.

## Presumptive Claims

Some of you may be filing for "presumptive" benefits. Claims involving Veterans who were prisoners of war, exposed to nuclear testing, asbestos, or herbicides are accorded certain presumptions. These Veterans need only prove by records that they actually were where they say they were, and the risk is automatically assumed. Thus, if all the conditions are met, no nexus letter is needed for service connection. The medical records are all that is needed to support it. A denial at this juncture isn't unheard of but usually involves a misunderstanding of the regulations on VA's part. One Veteran exhibited signs of diabetes prior to service in Vietnam. This was noted in his SMRs. When he claimed a presumptive for DM2 associated with Agent Orange exposure, he was denied, and this was upheld on appeal. It was quite obvious it wasn't a result of AO. Keep this in mind when you file. A Vet filed for PTSD and said he was in combat. The records showed he was a cook and nowhere near any enemy action. He lost too. Continuity is important. Another Vet's operating base was attacked by the Viet Cong. He was a clerk/typist, and VA denied him. The BVA used the Joint U.S. Center for Research of Uniformed Records (JUSCRUR) to find out that everyone on the base defended it just as he said he did. He won. It took 5 years.

I had a Veteran ((WGM) who followed my "recipe" from my blog site and was denied for hepatitis based on STDs proving willful misconduct. STDs are *not* considered such, and the denial was overturned within several months. He had filed the claim based entirely on jet guns and had the best evidence I have ever seen assembled. Oddly, VA had made the "finding" that the STDs were the cause of his disease, and they could not rescind that. It was cast in stone. This is called a finding. They were forced into granting his claim even though he had no nexus tying the venereal disease to the hepatitis. This is rare, but it happens. I strongly suspect they did not relish the idea of doing battle with him over the jet gun risk because he clearly would have won with four nexus letters.

# B
# New and Material Evidence Submittal

Because the delay between filing and denial is so long, you often will come into possession of more evidence while you are waiting for news. You may want to hold on to this and see if you win without it. Circumstances vary from one Vet to another. It may be the smoking gun that will help you win. A "buddy letter" is a classic example. This is new and material evidence that may help win the claim. You may decide to send it in immediately or hold it back and wait for a decision. If they deny, this can be submitted to reopen the denial and start a new decision process. It happens fairly quickly too.

New and material evidence, as defined by the Court, is this. "New" means it has never been submitted before. "Material" means it has bearing on the claim and may be helpful in proving your contentions. The definition has been fought over for several decades, and the meaning has seesawed back and forth. Currently, the Vet has the high ground on this one. 38 CFR §3.156(a) defines it as:

2) **General.** A claimant may reopen a finally adjudicated claim by submitting new and material evidence. New evidence means existing evidence not previously submitted to agency decisionmakers. Material evidence means existing evidence that, by itself or when considered with previous evidence of record, relates to an unestablished fact necessary to substantiate the claim. New and material evidence can be neither cumulative nor redundant of the evidence of record at the time of the last prior final denial of the claim sought to be reopened, and must raise a reasonable possibility of substantiating the claim.

# C
# Appeals Time Limits
# Filing the Notice of Disagreement (NOD)

If you are denied, you will have a year to file your Notice of Disagreement (NOD) with the denial. You also may submit new and material evidence that will require an all new decision-making process based on it and your prior initial filings. This does not affect the one year date. That is counted from the last denial on file. Therefore, once you file new evidence to rebut the denial, VA has to start the clock over. VAROs have a long history of confusing any submissions. It will not be surprising if you file new evidence in a claim, and they try to treat it as a reopening of the claim you are currently pursuing. In the top right corner of all letters they mail you, there will be an "In reply, refer to _____." This will usually consist of a three-number/three-letter combination. Always use it. If you are denied again and are not filing any new evidence, you must now file the NOD to protect yourself. You don't want to milk this out over a lifetime, but if denied, you do have the avenue of continuing to send in new and material evidence to provoke yet another decision process.

## Filing the Notice of Disagreement (NOD)

**Things needed:** Form 21-4138 or your favorite paper substance.

Once you have presented all that you can and are still denied, the time for the NOD has come. This must say, at a minimum, your disagreement with the denial and a desire to obtain "appellate review." This is very important. If you do not say "request appellate review," it is whatever VA says it is. A complaint. A bitch letter. They do this. Trust me.

You should discuss why it is you are filing the NOD. This includes a brief discussion of what you have submitted so far. Tell them that proves your case and why their analysis is wrong. Any evidence that has been interpreted wrongly should be discussed, and a reason why it is wrong needs to become part of the record. If you are doing this with a VSO, make sure they include the phrase, "I request appellate review of this claim." Always identify yourself six ways to China and look for the "in reply, refer to" followed by three numbers/three letters in the upper right of your denial letter. More recently I have seen four--number, three letter combinations but it always says "In reply, refer to…".

A NOD does not have to be the Gettysburg address. It does need to cover every reason why VA came to the wrong conclusion supported by facts and the submitted evidence. Everything you submit or VA gets is called Evidence of Record (EOR). They will use this abbreviation, so look for it. Use it when you refer to something. If there is "negative evidence," point out why it isn't important. Always address every reason for the denial. If you leave one out, your Statement of the Case (SOC) will say, "Claimant failed to account for the documented marijuana usage during service. This affects his credibility, etc."

If you screwed up on your continuity, this is the time to fix it. Everything you are going to use to win has to go into this *one last time*. You cannot keep on adding things in later because it makes you look like you're inventing it as you go. VA will use that against you too.

# D

# DRO Hearing and Review?

If you feel something important is being ignored that would prove service connection, you are entitled to ask for a hearing before a decision review officer. I have had zero luck with them, and virtually, all the Vets I've helped said the same thing. They are stuck on one setting—deny. Choosing a DRO review and hearing will set your claims process back at least a year. With little to gain from it, I always suggest getting the claim to DC—the sooner the better. Most Vets do not understand the concept. If you have presented everything you have and they still deny, going in front of the DRO and pleading your case with the exact same evidence is pretty retarded. They are not going to "suddenly" see it your way. It's all based on evidence, not your capabilities in presenting it to them. You are also getting into a long line of other Vets who are doing the same thing. VSOs love to advocate this path because it keeps the adjudication local. They get to monkey with it longer. They reason that it is one more opportunity for a win, which can thus avoid an appeal. It is ultimately your choice, but statistics are not favorable when there is nothing more to submit in your defense. Asking for both a RO hearing and review will not preserve your place in line in Washington DC. Many times, your claim is so complicated from the VA examiner's perspective that they deny because they have never done one before or are afraid to screw it up. Jet gun claims are like this. Ninety-five out of one hundred of these will come to the conclusion that the evidence is too speculative to make a call. That's another way of denying it and punting on fourth and long.

Some Vets file a NOD with new and material evidence to rebut the VA's denial. I'm ambivalent about this. My desire has always been to get the process over with. VSOs are of a mind to milk this out forever and then proceed to a NOD. Either way works, but a NOD gets the ball rolling. A submission of new and material evidence without a NOD can provoke a new decision sooner. If VA has decided they are simply not going to grant, this will prove it. File the NOD with more evidence if you have it or a list of reasons as to why they're wrong and you're right. I like to file more evidence with the NOD, personally. I always hold something back for this. It has two effects. One, the clock starts again on a new adjudication, and two, the claim is now on its way to appellate status. If VA denies again, it will be followed almost immediately by the Statement of the CASE (SOC). The law says they cannot announce a denial in a SOC. This moves you down the field closer to the goalposts and starts a new decision process. You have accomplished two things at once. You have started the appeal process and also get a quick, new look at your claim. It's not cheating. It's just smart. Trust me.

Sometimes new and material evidence comes into your possession after you have filed your NOD. If this happens, send it in with a notation that you wish to have a new (*de novo*) adjudication based on the newly submitted evidence based on 38 CFR §3.156 (b):

> **Pending claim.** New and material evidence received prior to the expiration of the appeal period, or prior to the appellate decision if a timely appeal has been filed (including evidence received prior to an appellate decision and referred to the agency of original jurisdiction by the Board of Veterans Appeals without consideration in that decision in accordance with the provisions of § 20.1304(b) (1) of this chapter), will be considered as having been filed in connection with the claim which was pending at the beginning of the appeal period.

This will stop the clock again until they either grant or deny. If it (the submission of the new evidence) occurs *after* they have sent you a SOC or an SSOC, but before you have filed your Form 9, you should make sure VA understands this. They have often attempted to claim you did not file the Form 9 within the sixty days. To avoid having to fight this additional issue on appeal, make sure you use the "in reply to" number/alphabet combination you find on the SOC/SSOC. Certified Mail—RRR at this point is a must to protect your appeal.

In summary, let's recap. You have now been denied and filed your NOD. You may have chosen to go the DRO route for a review of your denial and/or a hearing to accompany it. If you have obtained new and material evidence, you have filed it and still been denied or are awaiting a new decision. Obviously, if you win now, proceed to chapter 5.

If you have submitted new and material evidence after your SOC, but before a DRO hearing or DRO review has occurred, VA will mail out a new letter either denying or granting the claim. If denied, it will soon be followed by a Supplemental Statement of the Case (SSOC). This is simply a SOC with an extra S in front of it. You may choose to answer it or proceed to the DRO. It is best to confirm your reservation for the hearing or DRO review. VA is very forgetful when it serves their purposes.

# E
# SOC and SSOC Time Limits

Once the SOC or the SSOC has been issued and you receive it, you do not want to delay. You must file your Form 9 within sixty (60) days of issuance of this document if you have nothing else to submit. This is where more claims get screwed up than I can count with VSOs. It sits on their desk, and you wait for a call. Nothing happens, and the suspense date comes and goes with no action. Sixty days can go by in the blink of the eye. VA knows this and counts on it. VSOs have lots of important things to do, such as getting new POAs in their pockets. Your claim is sometimes not as pressing and gets shuffled off to the side. This is why a pro se claim has more possibilities for success. You are in charge and you want to be prompt. There is no repair order if you miss this date. The only option is to refile and start over. If this happens, you will need new and material evidence to reopen. This might be in short supply, which will prevent you from reopening the claim. Do not let this happen.

I suggest filing the NOD sooner rather than later for several reasons. The VA is *sloooow*. It will be a year before they get the SOC out to you. In that time, you can begin assembling more evidence. If you can find it, get a new nexus to go with the old one (which is new and material, I might add) and remodel the kitchen. Time will weigh heavily on you. VA knows this. It can cause depression so be mindful of that. When they finally mail out this carbon copy of your denial (SOC), they will cite to all the pertinent regulations controlling the denial. This doesn't mean they considered them all. They just make you think they did. From this Statement of the Case, or SOC as it is known, you may now file the second half of your substantive appeal (Form 9), which will complete the process.

Why VA splits this appellate process in two is simple to me. They assume a certain percentage will grow weary of the process and give up. They are right. Many Vets file a NOD and never proceed further: 1.2 million file yearly and approximately 12 percent win. Of the denied, 350,000 maximum will file their NOD. Only forty-five thousand go on to appeal to the BVA. Of those, perhaps 23 percent win on appeal. Of the denied, five thousand will file a Notice of Appeal with the CAVC. As I mentioned earlier, fully 70 percent are remanded by the court back to the BVA for error or further action. The fact that we rarely see these Vets again on appeal leads us to believe VA struck some kind of bargain with them. Chances are that a determined Vet who goes up to the CAVC and gets a remand for more development and a new adjudication is not going to throw in the towel if he loses at the BVA again.

Keep in mind that you have sixty days from the date stamp of your SOC or SSOC to file the Form 9. If you are late, that's all she wrote. More Vets step on their necktie here than anywhere else. The choice of sixty days appears to be an arbitrary barrier with no reason. Considering we are always reminded that it is a nonadversarial process, it seems this part could be more open-ended like the 120-day time limit on appealing to the

CAVC. Until they change it, Vets and VSOs will continue to blow it off and then scratch their heads afterward. Don't be one of them.

# F

## Form 9s

### Filing the Form 9

**Things needed:** VA Form 9 and instructions or your own version. To avoid confusion, use theirs (http://www.rattler-firebird.org/va/forms/9.pdf) or carefully build your own and make sure to include each and every answer to the questions they ask in boxes one through nine.

The Form 9 is the big milestone in the claim. You are halfway through with a claim that should have been granted by now. You will file this either using their form or your own. I like computer paper, and I have no problem looking at what the VA wants stated. Blocks 1 through 7 are the usual name rank, airspeed, and tail number. Block 8 will ask if you would like a board hearing and, if so, where. If you live close to DC, you can ask for it there and get one rather soon. If you live in Maryland, this is where you go. You may also opt for a live hearing before a VLJ at your own VARO. If you want to speed up the claim, you may want to go for the videoconference link to a VLJ seated in DC. This is the fastest way and the one most used by Vets. Option number 4 is to waive your right to this and proceed to a decision.

Many trees have been cut down to print books on the subject of testifying in your own behalf. Remember that Shakespeare said, "A man who is his own lawyer has a fool for a client." Most attorneys cringe at the idea. In an ex parte format, this is not as dangerous as it sounds. A VLJ is not like Perry Mason and will not grill you on your lay testimony. He may ask the occasional question to clear up the concept in his mind. As this is tape recorded (when live) or videotaped, the judge can always go back and examine the testimony. I have seen this fix an error that is on paper many times. The judge is smart enough to see it. He does use twelve munchkins, but they are usually brighter than the life forms at the RO. I find you can get better justice if you can at least talk to the judge and let him see your intensity. This is definitely where a good impression and a clear reason for a grant are won. Having the law on your side is required, but falling inside the law's boundaries is sometimes as simple as explaining it in Dick and Jane speak. You have read what I have written about VA slanting the testimony to make absence of evidence appear to be negative evidence. Here is the place to point this out very clearly. Sometimes the spoken word does the trick where twenty pages of testimony don't.

I helped a lady get her Marine husband service connected in 2010 after six years of fighting. They were represented by the American Legion and were getting nowhere. He had HCV and a tattoo in Da Nang. The separation exam listed a tattoo on the right arm, and it was on the left. There was another on the right that had been surgically removed, and the scars proved it. VA denied because the tattoo was on the left arm. His first buddy letter was tossed as not being credible because of the long time interval (forty years). He got the second buddy letter from the pecker checker on board his ship and they tried to toss that one into the circular file. They did a videoconference with a nice judge, and the analog test was performed—he rolled up his sleeves, and there was the tattoo on the left and the remains of number 2 on the right. The VA had said the second buddy letter was no good because Pecker checker's mate, First Class Billy Bob Notadoctor, was never on the USS *Long Beach*. This untruth was resolved by submitting *his* DD214, which said down at the bottom that he was indeed aboard CGN-9. VA threw in the towel, and he won. I want you to know that he had an excellent nexus letter from his gastroenterologist that had all the i's and t's completed.

This didn't deter VA from being uncooperative. Sometimes they just won't give in until you talk to the man in charge. I often wonder what success his claim might have had if we could have been involved in the development of it right from the start. Tom would never have won without the videoconference. The RO never suggested he come in for confirmation. The denial would have been sustained at the BVA absent a simple viewing of the tattoo evidence. A picture is worth a thousand words—in court.

Block #9 states, "These are the issues I want to appeal to the VA." This seems self-explanatory. I have seen some of these from old C-files and mistakes are made. Recently, this came up in a case at the Court. They finally put a nail in it and said if you failed to list it in box #9, but discuss it in detail in box #10 or your attached reasons sheet, then you meant to appeal it. That was not the case ten years ago. If you did not specifically list each and every one, the unwritten ones were toast.

So you've listed the choice for a hearing, and you've identified the claims you want to appeal and the ones you wish to abandon. You've typed up a laundry list of everything they should have done and didn't. You have chosen the proper CFRs to cite for each disease/injury you claim. You can also look at decisions on the CAVC site for precedence if you have had time to investigate it. Add these to you reasoning. VA is obligated to look at all the evidence and give "reasons and bases" for what they decide pro or con. They are also required to look at every reason for an injury or disease—not just the ones you list.

The VA will pack up the file and send it surface mail, third class, slow boat via the Panama Canal. It will be a year before the BVA can tell you that that they actually have it in their hands. You can actually call them and ask (202-565-5436). You get to talk to someone who knows what's going on within three to four minutes. The difference between an RO and the BVA is amazing.

# G
# Hearing or No Hearing?

Carefully observe the Form 9. It has many blocks that require some action. Failure to fill one in can have disastrous results on what happens later.

You are filing the second half of your appeal. This is referred to as the "substantive appeal." The VARO will not read it. It is for the benefit of the BVA. You are now headed to DC, and the RO is finished with you. You may ask for a video hearing either in front of a live judge or a videoconference with one sitting in DC. Asking for the live version will increase the delay but will ensure you get to see the whites of his/her eyes. A picture may be worth a thousand words. A face-to-face with a judge who will decide your claim is one both of you will remember. If you are right and know it, it shows. If you are just a lazy bum looking for a nice pension to avoid working, the judge will figure this out. A Vet who is deserving and honest will make a tremendous impression. Always take your wife. Dress up for the occasion. A haircut and a shave are in order unless you feel the freak flag and Santa beard are your testimonial to individuality. Do not miss this auspicious occasion. Many Vets schedule this and forget to mark it on their calendar. If you do not show, it's supposed to be a simple oversight on your part. You can reschedule if you had a good excuse and told them ahead of time. An unexcused no-show is bad form, and VA will take that to mean you are not sufficiently motivated to defend your claim. For the record, I have never seen a Vet who skipped out on the hearing win. I recommend that Vets travel to the hearing the day before if it is more than fifty miles away. First, it gives you a reason to relax, get out into the fresh air, and have a nice dinner at a restaurant with Cupcake. Second, if there is some horrific automobile accident, it won't make you late. There is no "late" for these affairs. Either you're there, or you're not. My latest one was for 0900. I lived eighty miles away. We opted to arrive the evening before. We were rested and prepared the next morning and arrived early.

The receptionist sent us up at 0815 because the Vet in the 0800 time slot was a no-show. We got the judge early in the day before he was tired and irritable. This is a good thing to do if you can. Avoid a hearing time in the afternoon—especially after lunch—when the VLJ may be inclined to take a siesta mentally. There is method to this madness. Most people don't think it through. Some, but not all, VARO hearing schedulers will give you a little bit of a choice. Others simply inform you of when yours will transpire. If you are very ill because of your disease, you will be given more leeway.

Getting back to the Form 9, you will see a space (#8) to request a BVA hearing if you desire. You must check a box, or this will boomerang back for you to fill out again in several months when they finally notice it. Box #9 is very important. I cannot tell you how many claims have died on this mistake. Choose properly, or it will be the end of a claim you want to keep alive. If some of your claim has been deferred, I strongly suggest you still list it as desirous of appeal. The worst that can happen is that they will say it is not ripe for appellate review yet. Box #10 is not large enough for you to say one-tenth of what you hope to. My "box #10" was twenty pages long.

# H
## BVA Waiver of VARO Review

The last step is to add a waiver of RO review. Many pro se Vets forget to do this, and the VLJ may need to clear something up or make a ruling on it at the BVA. If you do not sign a waiver, they will remand it back to the RO for a new decision process, which can set you back another year or more. You don't want that. Assemble this package and take it to the post office for the green card treatment. Keep all your green cards in one file with a notation on each one describing what you sent in with it. If VA wants to get into a "he said…she said" with you, one thing will be clear from the timeline of filings. If you had sixty days to file the F-9 and you have a green card proving you mailed them something at that time, chances are it wasn't glossy 8.5 x 11s of your grandson.

There is no form for a Waiver of Review. I would use the form letter I created here:

> Dept of Vet Affairs
>
> Kansas VARO
>
> 1234 Yellowbrick Rd.
>
> Oz, Kansas 60609
>
> Today's Date
>
> Re: Joe Veteran
>
> File # C-123456
>
> SSN 123-45-6789
>
> **WAIVER OF REVIEW**
>
> To whom it may concern:
>
> I hereby relinquish my right to a review of any new evidence submitted to the VLJ or the Board of Veterans Appeals by the Agency of Original Jurisdiction (AOJ). I realize this allows the Veterans Law Judge to make a decision in my claim that is not reviewable by my Regional Office VA examiner in the first instance.
>
> Joe Vet printed name
>
> Signature

This is the last you will hear of your bottle in the ocean. The VA will pack up the file and find the absolute slowest method of mail to D.C. It will be a year before the BVA can tell you that that they actually have it in their hands. You can actually call them and ask. You get to talk to someone, who knows what's going on, within three to four minutes. The difference is amazing. A representative of the BVA may call in several years with a question, so keep your listed phone number the same. You can and should submit any new evidence you obtain as soon as you get it. The BVA will add this to the pile. I always send in another waiver of RO review on the off chance they employ Murphy's Law and do not look for the original waiver. Laugh if you will, but some of the simplest ommisions can have horrible consequences.

# I
# BVA Motions for Reconsideration

On the off chance that your claim has run up on the rocks because of a horrible miscarriage of justice, you have two alternatives. The first is a petition for a Motion for Reconsideration (MFR). The BVA is not required to do this. It is purely a decision on their part. A motion must be heard by more than the single judge who took your first appeal. To keep the odds of a tie from happening, the MFR must be heard by three VLJs. This decision to hear your case is made by the Office of General Counsel (OGC). If some major flaw is perceived (finally), they may opt to do this in a covert attempt to fix it. Oddly, they occasionally decide to do this without your asking them to. Of course, that's when you *know* something is amiss. Assuming they opt not to hear it, you have 120 sunrises to file a Notice of Appeal with the Court of Appeals for Veterans Claims (CAVC or the Court). This costs US$50 unless you file an indigent claim. In that case, it's zero.

# J
# CAVC
# The Court of Appeals for Veterans Claims

So here you are. You've fired all your guns, and nothing happened. I strongly suggest you seek out the services of a good VA lawyer if you feel your case holds water. The attorney will certainly tell you whether it's worth fighting for or not. You may appeal it up to the Court where it will be heard by a single judge. The filing fee is $50, and you can file a statement of indigence, which waives the fee. You can do this pro se, but it will require some intense studying on your part to nail down a good legal argument. I have met many Vets who have handled this without panicking. It's not that difficult because the VA is a closed system, and their rulings are on a finite number of subjects. You will need plenty of time to do it too. If this was the plan (pro se) all along, I will assume you have looked at plenty of BVA decisions to get a feel for how that worked. The same can be said about Court cases. Amazingly, you will see real logic employed. No longer will you read of rights trampled and evidence overlooked. These guys are on this like white on rice. No theory is too far-fetched to examine. Often, they find things wrong that you didn't see. If they do, you win. They will remand this down to the BVA or even the RO if they were the boneheads who screwed it up. This is where you will win if you possibly can. One word of caution. Every argument you make here has to be one you discussed at the BVA hearing. No brand new risk factors or stressors out of the blue.

They only need to find one thing wrong for a remand. If you list six and they find the first one is true, they won't even look at #2–6. Such is justice. The Court finds something wrong more than 60 percent of the time. With that knowledge, you can see they will find *most* errors. I say most. If it is a fine point of law or a new reading of an old regulation, they may rule against you. This means you can appeal to the Federal Circuit Court.

VA can see the writing on the wall. They are not going to invest a lot of time in defeating a claim with merit. The benefit of the doubt will usually surface, and you will begin a new battle for the correct ratings percent. The reason I say this is simple. The CAVC has a name attached to a claim, not a number. It's easy to keep track of how many times a Veteran makes the trip up there. Names are easy to find. If Skeezics S. Skidless has filed a claim and comes back, there will be two or more entries. The fact is that this is rare. It happens, but you can search the records and find fifteen or twenty instances over twenty-two years. Where did all those Vets get off to? My supposition is based on Occam's razor. The simplest explanation is most often the correct one. They won or VA sat down and did some horse trading with them. Vets have told me of VA DROs sitting down with their service officer and bargaining. They may grant for PTSD at 60 percent if you drop the claims for HCV, AIDS, cancer, and hemorrhoids. Often, the VA secretary and his minions will sit down with a CAVC claimant, and they will all come to a "mutual understanding" that everyone can live with. In cases like this there is paperwork signed to that effect. Read it carefully.

History is the best predictor of what will happen in a closed system like the VA judicial arena. It tells me that the longer you keep this claim alive, the greater the chance you will win. Either your C-file begins to have its own gravitational pull because of sheer volume, or a rater in your VARO throws up his hands and says, "Enough! I give in!" Whichever occurs is immaterial. The results are what count, and complaining seems to be the winning component.

A loss at this stage is indicative that your claim is really grasping at straws. If you feel yours honestly has merit, or if your lawyer does, he may choose to go on up a notch to the Federal Circuit. They too can refuse to hear it if there is nothing of legal substance to discuss. An appeal to the Supreme Court can be petitioned for, but rarely ever occurs.

Keep this in mind. When you get to the Court, the Veteran friendly environment in which to present your claims disappears. You are now in a struggle with the VA secretary on an equal footing. You no longer enjoy any perks of just being a Veteran. If you are pro se and do something incredibly dumb, it will cost you. The Court tries to be deferential to you but you are on your own. You do have the right to remain stupid.

This concludes the pursuit of denials. I do not contemplate you having to read these chapters because proper preparation is going to give you a win at the VARO. Winning is a state of mind that is translated into the muscle from the mind. Whether it is typing it up, remembering all the old details and facts, collecting the evidence, or simply waiting for justice, the mind has to constantly be evolving the winning plan. A goal has to be visualized to be realized. This is not a bunch of pep talk. It is a living claim that evolves as your knowledge of what you are doing does. I sure didn't have a clue when I broke loose from the Military Order of the Purple Heart. All I knew for certain was I couldn't do any worse that those who were trained to do it. You can too. If you run into a wall, my Web site is available, and so am I. In fact, this book is designed to be used with my website because a lot of what you need to win is there.

# K
## About the Court and How It Works

Up to this point, you have been accorded every consideration in what they call a Veteran-friendly environment. From here on out, that does not apply. If you are pro se, you can make a few mistakes, but you are not given any judicial considerations. The Court is not your buddy any more than the VA is. The big difference is they are not as biased.

The Court is not a part of the VA. They are completely independent and make a point of telling the VA secretary (VASEC) that fairly regularly. The Court is comprised of nine judges, and one vacancy is currently unfilled. This has been so for quite some time. The judges must be approved by the Senate. That requires a hearing and a lot of martinis. One of these days, they'll finish it, and we'll have a full crew. As it is now, they finally have enough to avoid bringing in the retired justices to keep up with the caseload and fill out enough seats for an *en banc* review.

If your case has no particular uniqueness or is not liable to upset any established law, it will be decided by a single judge. This will not be a precedent-setting decision. You have four possible outcomes here.

Your claim can be remanded for further development if the BVA forgot to do something correctly or you were denied due process. This is called vacating your claim and remanding it for a new adjudication from scratch before the RO or the BVA—whichever was the dummy that screwed up.

If the BVA really stepped on their necktie, the court has the option to reverse in your favor. This is a win. The judge will still remand it down to the RO, but that is simply for them to give you your rating. Reversals are usually based on a total misreading of the evidence of record (EOR). If the BVA ignored something that conclusively proves you won, reversal will happen. Most times they vacate and remand, though.

The third option is a loss. This is called an affirmation. The fourth, and last, is if your claim has the potential for disturbing established precedence, the case will be referred to a panel of three judges. Remember, a normal situation will be a single judge ruling. You will have to ask for this panel review and tell them why you feel it is appropriate. The results of this decision will be incorporated into law and held binding on all future claimants. If the case is earth-shattering and may cause decades of precedence to fall by the wayside, the court will convene *en banc* rather than as a panel of three. An *en banc* court consists of seven judges.

The Court is not a trier of fact but sometimes does. Their main job is to make sure no laws were broken in the pell-mell race to deny you. They do not ordinarily dig into the facts of your claim. If justice has very obviously been trampled, they reverse or vacate. This is a retrying of the facts in everything but name only. Reversals are rare but not unheard of. Every year, there seems to be one or two. The Court, in what was unarguably the most famous Veterans case—Gilbert v. Derwinski (1990)—held:

> "A finding is 'clearly erroneous' when although there is evidence to support it, the reviewing court on the entire

evidence is left with the definite and firm conviction that a mistake has been committed."

—United States v. United States Gypsum Co., 333 U.S. 364, 395 (1948).

This is what Veterans justice is all about in my book. We are accorded the right of the benefit of the doubt. That is no small advantage in any court.

The third option (loss) brings out another Notice of Appeal. It must occur within sixty days of your loss. This appeal is to the Third Federal Circuit Court of Appeals. Your appeal will be heard by a minimum of a panel of three. Again, the Federal Circuit is not a trier of fact. They too will examine the case for judicial error based on established law in place at the CAVC.

As long as the law was observed, there is no reason to hear this, and VA can move for dismissal. Most decisions at this level are reversals or affirmation of the court's finding. Some entail a remand for more development, but these are rare. Statistically, there are more wins than losses here for Vets. America has a soft spot for Vets, and judges hate to rule against us. There's a good reason for this. First, it's just bad form. Second, and most importantly, it's bad for recruitment morale. If young men and women get the impression that they are going to get no benefits after being injured in the service of their beloved country, they may not want to join up. This would provoke the draft again, and nobody wants that.

In the event you lose here, you have one last option. If you can convince the Supreme Court to hear you claim, you are still in business. This process is called a writ of certiorari. Very few are granted to Veterans. It's not that we are undeserving. Very little of our case law affects America. It's Veteran-oriented and has no impact on regular legal matters. This isn't true 100 percent of the time, but the occasional case that makes it there is usually appealed by VASEC. Yes, you read that right.

As odd as it may seem, the tables can turn if you win at the CAVC, and the VASEC is not pleased with the outcome. He has the option to appeal *his* loss (your win) to the Federal Circuit and on up to the Supreme Court if defeated there. As he represents the government, the Supremes often feel compelled to hear his gripe. The claim will always read Nod v. Shinseki until he appeals to the Federal Circuit. At that point, the claim becomes Shinseki v. Nod. I doubt that you or I will ever venture that high. If I do, I will be seeking legal representation.

This concludes your legal options for an original claim. There are other types of legal challenges available to you after final, unappealed denials. One is a motion for revision, otherwise known as a CUE filing. CUE "stands for clear and unmistakable error." You cannot file for this unless the statute of limitations has expired on a claim. The other option is a motion for reconsideration after the statute of limitations has expired. This is a poor option. It is a one shot deal. If you petition and they turn you down, that's the end of it. If they hear your case and decide against you, you have no right to appeal and it ends there too. It's a dead-end street and a lose-lose for Vets.

There are claims for increase that generally follow the same guidelines as what I have covered here, but again, once you have won, there is no battle to attain service connection. A claim for increase is based entirely on part 4 of the CFR and is simply a determination of which diagnostic code most closely matches your symptoms. In that regard, they are rather small potatoes after all we have covered here. This does not mean VA is lax in trying to hoodwink you or give you a bum steer. That part of their game is still very much alive.

# CHAPTER 5

## YOU WIN (OR DID YOU?)

### A
### What's Next?

Let's assume you have made your case at the RO and are granted service connection (SC). Congratulations! Your battle may have just begun. Each disease or injury is rated according to a schedule that has a ratings percentage. The diagnostic codes in part 4 of 38 CFR list all these, and I will give you a link to them: http://www.law.cornell.edu/cfr/text/38/4/subpart-B

What most do not expect is that VA raters tend to offer you an ice cream cone with a scoop or two of air. Regardless of what your medical records show, VA tends to take the view that it isn't nearly as bad as the doctors described. You may need to have your doctor write *another* letter that more fully describes your circumstances in "VA speak" to get a rating equal to your circumstances. This is par for the course. Be prepared for it. I suggest you avoid telling the raters what percent they owe you at this stage. I would list all the ailments or symptoms based on what is truthful and documented and make sure they know this. They're dense, but at this stage the meanness has been set aside, and you have won. You are treated with far more respect once you are inside the wire. VA may choose to send you out for their C&P exam to measure your injury. At this point, they don't trust anyone. They lost and they want to do this one last time. Because they hate to just give you all that you should get up front, they give it in little pieces.

A classic example is diabetes type 2. VA will generally give you 10 percent for it, unless you can prove it is worse. They will agree to 20 percent without too much objection if properly documented but often dig their heels in when you ask for 40 percent. The semantics of the ratings language are full of "ifs," and some require multiple symptoms to move up to the next level. Other disease processes are couched in either/or language. Each is different, and some diseases include two entirely different sets of symptoms. You will need to become familiar with both the requirements as well as the phraseology of your disease in order to prevail. With hepatitis, the failure of the doctor to use the exact phrase "near-constant debilitating symptoms" can be the difference between 60 percent ($1,102/mo.) and 100 percent ($2,924/mo.). This is standard for VA and another of their little tricks you will need to navigate. Familiarize yourself, get the needed wording into the records, and present it. Better yet, have it in there before you submit the claim. VA examiners are *dense*, so this may or may not be recognized right away. When it happens, a simple follow-up letter in the form of a Notice of Disagreement (NOD) will often clear it up.

Hearing disorders are by far the worst example of VA's habits of lowballing. Tinnitus tops out at 10 percent. As for physical hearing loss, the total loss of hearing in one ear is not grounds for a 30 or 40 percent rating. Quite the contrary. You have to be virtually deaf in one ear and well on your way on the other ear to begin collecting a compensable amount. VA thinks that's what hearing aids are for. Or eyeglasses. Or wheelchairs. Or glass eyeballs like Tom Sellick's, etc.

Occasionally, one claim will be approved, and others will be deferred.

If you file a NOD, make sure any other claims are mentioned and that you still intend to prosecute them. If you don't, VA has been known to take the position that they thought you were abandoning them because you failed to mention them specifically. This is called "deemed denial". After one year of no action, they can say it's toast. Always remember you are dealing with lawyers. Their job is to win too.

You may have to take a claim up to the BVA on appeal if VA refuses to grant the rating you feel is deserved. VA will pay the lower rate while it is in appeal status, so do not feel you will be on hold until a resolution is arrived at. Many a claim goes to the CAVC when the BVA relies too heavily on the RO's assessment. Appeal it. The Court will see the game for what it is. I have described that process in an earlier chapter on denials. Often, the VARO will wait until the appeal is already in DC or virtually there and then cave in. I think it has something to do with the game of chicken or who's going to blink first. Insurance companies do this all the time. They see you are willing to go to court and intercept you at the front door. This is when they give you another, higher rating.

While you have been waiting for all those months for this win, I hope you followed my advice and started reading up on this. You want to get the best and highest ratings that are supported by the facts. Let's look at diabetes 2. It's listed under Diagnostic Code 7913 in part 4.119 (http://www.law.cornell.edu/cfr/text/38/4/119).

First, notice I have emphasized some of the ands, pluses, and ors. The reason is to show that some ratings require one set of symptom or another. Some require several. Where DM2 is concerned, you may have one set or another. They therefore accord you some leeway as to which you have and don't have.

> Requiring more than one daily injection of insulin, restricted diet, **and** regulation of activities (avoidance

of strenuous occupational and recreational activities) with episodes of ketoacidosis **or** hypoglycemic reactions requiring at least three hospitalizations per year or weekly visits to a diabetic care provider, **plus** either progressive loss of weight and strength **or** complications that would be compensable if separately evaluated ----------------100%

Requiring insulin, restricted diet, and regulation of activities with episodes of ketoacidosis **or** hypoglycemic reactions requiring one or two hospitalizations per year **or** twice a month visits to a diabetic care provider, **plus** complications that would not be compensable if separately evaluated-------------------------------------------------------- 60%

Requiring insulin, restricted diet, and regulation of activities----------------------------------------------------------- 40%

Requiring insulin and restricted diet, or; oral hypoglycemic agent and restricted diet ------------------------------------ 20%

Manageable by restricted diet only----------------------- 10%

Note (1): Evaluate compensable complications of diabetes separately unless they are part of the criteria used to support a 100 percent evaluation. Noncompensable complications are considered part of the diabetic process under diagnostic code 7913.

There is no rating for 0 percent. Either you have DM2, and it causes you problems or it doesn't. This is a presumptive disease if you were in Vietnam—even for one day. Vets get SC for this if they can prove they landed and took off three hours later for Bangkok. I think that's ludicrous. None of the Ranch Hand aircraft that sprayed herbicides were assigned there. They operated out of Bien Hoa Air Base.

Getting 10 to 20 percent for this is normal. The jump to 40 percent is where VA gets anal. Many Vets I have helped have had two of the three listed symptoms and lost. This is appealable on a narrow rationale. If your symptoms more closely approximate the higher ratings but you do not have all, there is some leeway accorded the rater. You have to push them to this conclusion by quoting 38 CFR §4.21:

> In view of the number of atypical instances it is not expected, especially with the more fully described grades of disabilities, that all cases will show **all** the findings specified. Findings sufficiently characteristic to identify the disease and the disability therefrom, and above all, coordination of rating with impairment of function will, however, be expected in all instances.

And §4.7:

> Where there is a question as to which of two evaluations shall be applied, the higher evaluation will be assigned if the disability picture more nearly approximates the criteria required for that rating. Otherwise, the lower rating will be assigned.

Veterans need to know that symptoms listed in the diagnostic code are simply meant for guidance and not an exhaustive list. Thus, with a requirement for insulin and a required diet and "some" restriction of activities self-described by the Vet, he should be eligible for 40 percent. VA is adamant about this. If you do not have a signed letter from your doctor that specifically restricts your activities, you will never advance past 20 percent. Some Vets are unaware of this and make no attempt to find out what they can get. They blindly trust their VSO or VA doctor to do the right thing. Nobody is going to tell you this at the VA. You have to be proactive to get anything. Knowledge of your disease/injuries and the ratings schedule covering it is a must. Most find this out when they get the denial letter. Your VSO will usually say he didn't know or that he's never seen this happen before. You should not have to pay for his ignorance of the law.

When you win, they go through a ratings procedure that examines your medical records carefully to give you a rating. VA is going to try to low-ball you in hopes you won't complain or are ignorant of what you are legitimately entitled to. When you write back and explain that they misread your medical records and include new ones with your highlighter pen all over the parts needed to get the higher rating, they will comply. It's a test to see how dumb you are. All raters aren't this way, but enough are to give them all a bad reputation. You are not advised to tell them how to do this, just that you are underrated and why. I always push the envelope but do it politely.

VA has another ratings rule against pyramiding or piling ratings on top of ratings where you end up duplicating what you claim for a higher percentage (38 CFR §4.14):

> The evaluation of the same disability under various diagnoses is to be avoided. Disability from injuries to the muscles, nerves, and joints of an extremity may overlap to a great extent, so that special rules are included in the appropriate bodily system for their evaluation. Dyspnea, tachycardia, nervousness, fatigability, etc., may result from many causes; some may be service connected, others, not. Both the use of manifestations not resulting from service-

connected disease or injury in establishing the service-connected evaluation, and **the evaluation of the same manifestation under different diagnoses are to be avoided**.

What VA does not tell you is where this *is* permitted. You have to investigate it yourself and determine if this is possible. Here is an example. I have porphyria cutanea tarda (PCT). The rating for this is under §4.118 (the skin): http://www.law.cornell.edu/cfr/text/38/4/118. PCT is listed under DC 7815. It permits a rating of 10 percent for scarring:

> At least 5 percent, but less than 20 percent, of the entire body, or **at least 5 percent, but less than 20 percent, of exposed areas affected, <u>or</u>**; intermittent systemic therapy such as corticosteroids or other immunosuppressive drugs required for a total duration of less than six weeks during the past 12-month period ---------------------------------- 10%

There are many Vets who have to get phlebotomies for this. They remove a pint of blood and throw it in the trash can because it's contaminated. There is no rating for phlebotomies in DC 7815 so you have to search through the various codes to find it listed somewhere. Polycythemia vera DC 7704 has just this—specifically, a rating for phlebotomies:

> Requiring phlebotomy --------------------------------------- 40%

This is the only listing for phlebotomies anywhere in the Diagnostic Code, so you can ask for it and get it without an argument. What you can also do is collect the 10 percent for the scarring under DC 7815 because you are not duplicating (pyramiding) symptoms. This is light-years beyond what VSOs are capable of. Veterans can explore all manner of these little tricks that work in their favor. I suggest getting all the big ratings service connected before experimenting with some of these cutting edge interpretations.

One that is now becoming more important to Iraqi Vets is pain. You can be rated for your injuries and get the rating equal to the injury. What isn't included is the pain experienced. VA is legally required to rate that as a separate component if it is not discussed in the assigned rating.

Look at these two regulations. They deal with this subject, but raters and VSOs seem to zoom right over them without absorbing the meaning:

http://www.law.cornell.edu/cfr/text/38/4/40. 38 CFR §4.40 says:

> Disability of the musculoskeletal system is primarily the inability, because of damage or infection in parts of the system, to perform the normal working movements of the body with **normal excursion, strength, speed, coordination and endurance**. It is essential that the examination on which ratings are based adequately portray the anatomical damage, and the functional loss, with respect to all these elements. The functional loss may be due to absence of part, or all, of the necessary bones, joints and muscles, or associated structures, or to deformity, adhesions, defective innervations, or other pathology, **or it may be due to pain, supported by adequate pathology and evidenced by the visible behavior of the claimant undertaking the motion. Weakness is as important as limitation of motion, and a part which becomes painful on use must be regarded as seriously disabled.** A little used part of the musculoskeletal system may be expected to show evidence of disuse, either through atrophy, the condition of the skin, absence of normal callosity or the like.

With this in your records, you can ask for an extra schedular rating for pain. It is perfectly legitimate, and VA should have to compensate you for it. Simply having a part of your foot missing will get you *X* percent. Getting a rating for the pain that is not factored in is necessary and perfectly legal.

38 CFR §4.45 covers pain in subsection (f):

> **(f)** Pain on movement, swelling, deformity or atrophy of disuse. Instability of station, disturbance of locomotion, interference with sitting, standing and weight-bearing are related considerations. For the purpose of rating disability from arthritis, the shoulder, elbow, wrist, hip, knee, and ankle are considered major joints; multiple involvements of the interphalangeal, metacarpal and carpal joints of the upper extremities, the interphalangeal, metatarsal and tarsal joints of the lower extremities, the cervical vertebrae, the dorsal vertebrae, and the lumbar vertebrae, are considered groups of minor joints, ratable on a parity with major joints. **The lumbosacral articulation and both sacroiliac joints are considered to be a group of minor joints, ratable on disturbance of lumbar spine functions.**

Searching through part 4 is like getting a free pass in the candy store when you have a rating. Your imagination is your only drawback. VA isn't going to welcome you with open arms, and they will resist it if they have never seen it done before. I spotted the phlebotomy rating trick in a BVA decision from 1998 while I was waiting for my decision. I tried it after I won, and they didn't even argue. If you don't try it, you'll never know. Please do not expect VA to volunteer to rate you for it.

Now having said all this, there is a logical point of no returns. Once you have gone over 100 percent plus an additional 60 percent special monthly compensation S (housebound), you can get no more money unless you are severely debilitated and on your last legs. Vets at that stage need constant care and are awarded Aid and Attendance Rate at different rates. Additionally, if you have lost the use of some appendages like both legs, arms, are blind, are blind and deaf or combinations of all of these, you will move into special monthly compensations (SMCs), such as L, L ½, M, M ½, N, N ½, O/P, R.1, and R.2. It is possible for a Vet with spouse to get $8,080/month under R.2.

Just because you haven't seen it happen doesn't mean it can't be done. Vets go before the CAVC all the time with "what ifs" such as these. The law is so unexplored that new interpretations of what you are entitled to are being discovered every year. Remember, Veterans Law is only 23 years old.

If you appeal a rating and are denied, you will have to file a NOD and begin the process again. It isn't nearly as obnoxious this time. If you just got a new rating and are appealing it, your request for a higher one will be handled promptly. They will act on it and give it to you if your records can support it. If not, it's off to DC. VA will try to meet you halfway on this if it is plausible. If it looks like a new concept, they'll punt and let the BVA be the guinea pigs. Now with that said, I read a lot of BVA decisions, and I have seen almost none where a Vet's claim came back up to the VLJ for a higher initial rating. This leads me to believe that somebody shook hands with somebody in the hallway at the RO. This is often where promises are made and gifts are exchanged.

Appealing a rating all the way to the CAVC is identical to what you experience when trying to win initially. Often, when VA sees you are prepared to take it up the ladder, they will wait until the last moment and suddenly grant it. I have no explanation for why. I just observe that they seem to do it a lot. If you simply accept what they give you when you finally win, you're stuck with it. If you appeal as soon as possible and show them you don't drive turnip wagons for a living, they give you more. Don't be afraid to do this. I don't know how many Vets I have talked to who say they got 0 percent for tinnitus in 1996 but were afraid to upset the applecart and ask for the 10 percent when they won Service Connection (SC). I have a newsflash for you. Some of these old wives' tales are perpetuated by VSOs. VA wants you to tremble and say, "Thank you, Sir." Vets who don't complain make the rater's job easier. We don't want that.

## B
## Fenderson or Staged Ratings

If you filed in 2000 and finally win in 2012, you probably got worse over the intervening years. When this happens, VA will not tell you that you are entitled to a sliding scale rating that rises as your symptoms increase. This must be confirmed by contemporaneous medical records. What this means is that a back injury worth 20 percent a month gradually became a 40 percent one. It conceivably made life a complete wreck over time, and you are now totally disabled and unable to work. You can ask for a Fenderson rating named after who else, but Mr. Joseph Fenderson. He was the first one to try this, and he won at the CAVC. This is very important to you. VA tends to just give you a low rating without doing the homework. The time to ask for this is when you win, not after ten years when you come back for an increase. VA has ruled that a staged rating can only be done with the initial claim. If a Vet is timid and coerced by his VSO to "leave well enough alone and not be greedy," he/she will miss out on something they are entitled to. It happens often enough that I think you should be aware of it.

Just because I taught you how to win doesn't means I'm going to abandon you. I have a bone to pick with the VA, and I'm letting you help do it. All these tips are focused on that idea.

# C
# You Win in DC

Let's assume you have finally struck gold in D. C. and are patting yourself on the back. You have no idea what's in store for you now.

Back the boat back up to the dock, Gilligan. Yes, you won, but what, exactly? You are not going to see what's behind door number 3 yet because the BVA has only made a decision in the affirmative. Now your claim and files must be packed up with tender, loving care and securely transported back to your local Regional Office. This will take a lot less time than VA took to send it to DC. When it arrives (about a month), they will review the medical records and make a decision on a rating percentage. Sometimes they send you out for a C&P to get the low down. Trust me when I said earlier that they are more optimistic about your health than your doctor is. When you get your new rating, you will probably be forced to file your NOD and begin this process all over again. You can file new medical evidence to rebut their decision. This will occur fairly rapidly (several months) as by now they are very tired of hearing your name. Lori and Tom got his win back from DC in early August 2010 and had his 100 percent P & T rating accomplished (up from an initial 60 percent) by late October. Rob won his and is still fighting them. Both Rob and Tom are stage 4 and should be on a par with one another claims wise.

VA has some mental defect that prevents them from just giving you what you deserve. All too often they hold back and tease you. If you know the ratings tables, you can see this. Few Vets learn this knowledge and instead rely entirely on their VSOs for this expertise. If your VSO service officer is mentally challenged, then your rating is going to suffer. If he knows nothing, he can hardly counsel you on your options.

Vets who operate pro se usually have a much better working knowledge of the VA rules and regulations because they have to in order to do this.

There certainly isn't any voodoo involved. You will have enough knowledge to do this, either with a VSO you can babysit, or by yourself if you wish. The choice is yours, but at least you have a choice. The knowledge learned here will protect you against ignorance and things that will harm your claim. Besides, there is always my website.

As you have read the paragraph above, I don't need to go into what you will need to fight for the correct rating.

# D
## Attaining 100 Percent Schedular Ratings

During the ratings dance to get one equal to your symptoms, you will have to assess whether you are totally disabled. This can be done by reading the ratings tables sometimes. Some diseases like hepatitis C have notes at the bottom of the ratings column that are innocent and do not really tell you much. When you file for the 100 percent, VA will drag out *their* book and say you aren't there yet. You do not want to file and then learn afterward what you lacked to win. That will really make it more time-consuming and difficult. Usually, each code will have these notes, and they vary from disease to injury.

At the bottom of HCV Diagnostic Code 7354 are two notes:

> Note (1): Evaluate sequelae, such as cirrhosis or malignancy of the liver, under an appropriate diagnostic code, but do not use the same signs and symptoms as the basis for evaluation under DC 7354 and under a diagnostic code for sequelae. (See § 4.14.)
>
> Note (2): For purposes of evaluating conditions under diagnostic code 7354, "incapacitating episode" means

a period of acute signs and symptoms severe enough to require bed rest and treatment by a physician.

Note #1 seems pretty clear unless you also suffer from cirrhosis of the liver. If you filed for that as well as the HCV, you will discover a new twist. VA will be inclined to apply the pyramiding clause at your expense. The catch 22 kicks in when they rate both claims. The symptoms list is almost identical at the lower ratings, so VA gives you the two lowest in each code to avoid the issue. You may be 100 percent by the DC 7354 code, but if they try to give you what you legitimately deserve for the cirrhosis, the conflict begins. I tell Vets to concentrate on the HCV rating at the expense of the cirrhosis (DC 7312) because the symptoms list is much more demanding for the higher cirrhosis rates.

Another ploy to get to 100 percent is to use 38 CFR §4.16 (TDIU) as the basis for an argument that it specifically says multiple illnesses attributable to a single disease process must be considered together:

> For the above purpose of one 60 percent disability, or one 40 percent disability in combination, **the following will be considered as one disability:** (1) Disabilities of one or both upper extremities, or of one or both lower extremities, including the bilateral factor, if applicable, (2) **disabilities resulting from common etiology** or a single accident, (3) **disabilities affecting a single body system**, e.g. orthopedic, **digestive,** respiratory, cardiovascular-renal, neuropsychiatric.

Note #2 says nothing about having a doctor's diagnosis in your medical charts stating that you have "near-constant debilitating symptoms." It simply talks about incapacitating episodes. As you approach the 40 percent rating, you will notice that the period of time that you are "incapacitated" or no longer able to work increases. You must document this by a time card or a doctor's nexus saying as much. If you hope to get the 100 percent rating, you will need a letter or notation in your medical record that says exactly that—"near constant debilitating symptoms." I have had three Vets hit that wall despite my warning them. It does no good to say it yourself. The doctor has to state it. In 2012, the CAVC also decided a case that specifically said HCV's diagnostic code does not specify a doctor's statement to that effect but does require it for back injuries. http://asknod. wordpress.com/2012/02/07/cavc-wisniewski-v-shinseki/

The VA has not said a word about weight loss other than to mention it in the ratings code as "minor" or "substantial." Yes, there's a regulation that defines that too. You won't see it until the denial either. Look at 38CFR §4.112, Weight Loss (http://www.law.cornell.edu/cfr/text/38/4.112), and there it is:

> For purposes of evaluating conditions in § 4.114, the term **"substantial weight loss" means a loss of greater than 20 percent of the individual's baseline weight, sustained for three months or longer;** and the term **"minor weight loss" means a weight loss of 10 to 20 percent of the individual's baseline weight, sustained for three months or longer.** The term "inability to gain weight" means that there has been substantial weight loss with inability to regain it despite appropriate therapy. **"Baseline weight" means the average weight for the two-year-period preceding onset of the disease.**

I don't want you to think the VA is mean, nasty, and conniving; but they are. If you have not wandered through this process before, they will cut you to pieces. When you start over or try to fix it, they complain and say you're trying to game the system. The need to get this right the first time is all-important. If you have an injury to a muscle group or groups from a shell fragment wound (SFW), read the whole section on the subject. Examine each and every Diagnostic Code in the section and search for these little notes and regulations that control your rating. VA does not make it easy, and if you are doing it pro se, you usually have no one to turn to and ask. Some VSOs are good, but they are only good on basics like win or lose. Sometimes they aren't even good at that. My Web site can alert you to much of this, as I have written and continue to write about these tricks extensively.

# E
# Total Disability Due To Individual Unemployment or TDIU

**Things needed:** http://www.rattler-firebird.org/va/forms/218940.pdf or your own letter on SF8.5x11 that covers everything on their form.

There will come a time when you hit the wall. It may be that a combination of your disabilities will make you incapable of employment. No single rating or combination of ratings will reach the magic 100 percent, but you still can't work. VA understands this and has a program to deal with it. TDIU will be granted if you qualify for one of these two scenarios:

(1) You have a rating of at least 60 percent or more for one disability and are physically unable to work; or
(2) You have a rating of at least 40 percent for one disability, but combined with other ratings, equals 70 percent or more and are unable to work.

This usually isn't granted until much later in life. Simply filing for it is no guarantee even if you have the requisite ratings. If VA determines you have two years of college, they'll declare you are capable of sitting in a chair and typing something. The key to this is if it is meaningful work. If you used to knock off $125 K a year as a bank manager, typing for $12/hour with no medical is not meaningful work. Vets with PTSD are often granted TDIU at an earlier age because of the effects of the mental illness. Other mental illnesses are treated similar to this too. Often, the key is the term "unable to work". You must prove this and your doctor is the key.

What VA does not tell you about TDIU is that you will be required to submit to a physical every once in a while to determine if you are still incapacitated. Some Vets with PTSD get better and are given a reduced percentage. Someone with rheumatoid arthritis starts a new medication, and the disease retreats. VA will reduce the rating, and it may go below the minimum needed to keep the TDIU. If VA finds out you are working, even under the table for cash, the party's over.

## F
## Going for Permanent and Total

Under normal circumstances, you will gradually get worse over time. Whether it's a disease or injury, the day will come where you simply can't work anymore. When VA finally grants you TDIU or 100 percent schedular, they will hold back the most important entitlement. I speak of the Permanent and Total rating. TDIU or 100 percent will give you the right to go shopping at the BX/PX commissary at the nearest military base. It makes no difference if you were Navy or Army. You are allowed to go on any base to access this. You are also allowed to use special services and rent airplanes, boats, jet skis, etc. You will have access to discount tickets for Disneyland/World and other venues in places like Orlando. The list is long, and new things are added all the time. Your U.S. government

ID card will save you 15 percent on donuts at Krispy Kreme, 10 percent at Home Depot, 5% at Cabela's, etc.

When you achieve the TDIU or 100 percent, VA will inform you that you will be scheduled for a new examination in two years to find out if you have gotten better or worse. If you get better, your rating may be lowered. If you have gotten worse or held your ground, VA will give you the P&T. P&T gives the GI bill to your spouse and children. It's called chapter 35, Dependents Education Allowance, or simply DEA. This is the goal. DEA will pay for forty-five months of college education for your spouse and each and every one of your dependents. Most states will also grant them free tuition for the same period, so the total effect is a free college education. The allowance for full time is $965/month right now. VA prorates it downward if they are attending part time. The benefits expire on your offspring' twenty-fifth birthday unless you/they petition for more time. Your spouse has twelve years. You as the Vet were supposed to use your own benefits for college years ago, so do not expect to collect too.

I read a lot and found a way to speed up the process and avoid the two-year wait. I had my doctor write a letter. What could be simpler? He stated that I was terminally ill, and there was no medical procedure or science that was going to turn the process around. I submitted my request for P&T and included the letter and three months later was granted the big banana. This is perfectly legal and above board. VA has to act on the request within three months, and they did.

There is a big difference between TDIU and 100 percent P&T. I mentioned above that if you are ever caught working while on TDIU, it will result in a forfeiture of your rating. This is not true of 100 percent scheduler ratings. You may legally work and earn as much as you want with the rating.

VA compensation is nontaxable. You may collect both compensation and SSI/SSD at the same time with no consequences. You may choose VA pension over SSI/SSD, but you cannot collect both. Most do because it is more than SSI. Veterans who served during a time of war are entitled to collect a VA pension after age sixty-five. You *will* need to prove that your service-connected and non–service-connected injuries are equal to or greater than 100 percent.

One last thing. I have spoken of percentages and what is needed to get to TDIU. VA math is very different that your daddy's math. Twenty percent + 20 percent does not equal 40 percent. To find out how weird it is, go to chapter 4, section 4.25: http://www.law.cornell.edu/cfr/text/38/4/25. The first thing you may notice is it will take twenty-two 10 percent ratings to get to 100 percent. That's a lot of tinnitus, hammer toes, hemorrhoids, and narcissistic mental disorders. I've seen some try it, but that isn't what I'm trying to teach here. This is for people with genuine claims that threaten your financial life as well as your physical one. I do not mean to be critical. I wrote this for those of you who, through no fault of your own, are severely injured. Some may use it as a guide to get service connected for any number of minor ills. I wish all of you luck. VA makes it very difficult.

# CHAPTER 6

## CLEAR AND UNMISTAKABLE ERROR (CUE) FILINGS

On occasion, you may discover an error on an old rating. You may have been denied for a claim in 1990, and while you are waiting on the new back claim to be decided, you find a glaring error in the old one. You can, under extremely limited instances, have this reversed. I would always suggest doing it with a lawyer, but some who read this will not be deterred. Once you get the hang of riding a bike, a motorcycle is no harder.

Clear and unmistakable error has been described as an outcome determinative error. It is one that later reviewers can see and recognize as such. It must consist of three things to qualify. First, the correct facts, as they were known, were not before the adjudicator, or the statutory rules and regulations were not followed. Second, the error must be undebatable. Therefore, a manifestly different outcome (a win) must be obvious if the error had not occurred. And third, the error must be based on the statutes and regulations that were in place at the time of the adjudication being attacked.

CUE is a knife fight in a dark alley between you and VA. There is no benefit of the doubt. There is no Veteran-friendly atmosphere. You are calling VA out and saying they screwed up. Either a mistake happened, or it didn't. There isn't a polite misunderstanding here.

If you cannot prove that a different outcome would have occurred, this is dead in the water. VA has taken a few arguments off the table. One is the duty to assist. If you asked for records to be obtained and VA didn't do it, their take is that you should have appealed it. As of 1993, you can no longer claim that. Now, if the Veterans Law Judge (VLJ) gave an incomplete reason or basis for your denial, that is CUE. If he played doctor and made a medical diagnosis, ditto. Some errors in 2012 look mighty stupid but the catch is whether it changed the outcome. Congress created the new CAVC (then the COVA) in 1989, and it took a few years to get straightened out. In that time, many BVA boards (panels of three) still had a doctor. Old habits die hard after thirty years too. Many errors occurred then.

Some still occur even today. Last March in Houston, one of the Vets I was helping get service connection for hepatitis wrote me that the RO had decided his HCV was because of six STD infections in service. They also declared it was willful misconduct (it isn't), and they weren't paying. He filed his NOD, and they relented and eventually granted HCV at 60 percent. Following my advice, he went on to 100% P&T several months later. It happens, but it's rare. I have only read of twenty or thirty successful ones in BVA decisions since 1992.

When filing a CUE, you must be horribly specific. You must put forth *each and every* item you feel was an error, what it was based on, and why the outcome would have been different but for the error. Every perceived error must be pled with specificity. If you do not bring it up, VA is not required to point it out. Simply arriving and mumbling the magic word CUE isn't enough.

VA does not help you win this kind of claim. They are your adversaries. They do not want you to win and will fight hard to defeat you. Their good name is at stake. Admitting error is very difficult for them. They are lawyers.

I suggest a lawyer if you want to fight VA this way. It's very difficult to win, and a lawyer can decide whether CUE exists and if it can be won.

# CHAPTER 7

## EARLIER EFFECTIVE DATE VIA 38 CFR §3.156(c)

One and only one avenue other than CUE is available to revisit an old decision. Let's say you are digging in the old Army footlocker and come across the medical records file you thought VA or the NPRC lost. Perhaps the army gave it to you forty years ago, and you just disremembered.

These are what we call "official service medical records." If there is something in them that will help prove your illness or injury, you can get the earliest date you ever filed for it. Guard them.

Let me give you an example. You file in 1990 for a back injury in service. VA sends off to the NPRC, and they say, "Sorry, Charlie. No medical records." VA does the claim, but you lose because there just isn't any evidence to prove it. Fast forward to 2010. You're cleaning out the garage, and you find the SMRs. First thing is to rent a safety deposit box. Next, reopen the claim and submit these documents. Keep your originals.

The rules are simple to get your old 1990 filing date and a lot of back pay. The newly discovered records must prove your case. In other words, the records must be the reason you win a new filing. There are a lot of reasons why records turn up later. Sometimes they were classified past the date you filed on. They may have been misplaced or left at the last base hospital where you were stationed. Vets should not care *how* it happened but *what* it will mean.

Here's how 38 CFR §3.156(c) is written:

> **Service department records. (1)** Notwithstanding any other section in this part, **at any time after VA issues a decision on a claim, if VA receives or associates with the claims file relevant official service department records that existed and had not been associated with the claims file when VA first decided the claim, VA will reconsider the claim,** notwithstanding paragraph (a) of this section. Such records include, but are not limited to:
>
> **(i) Service records that are related to a claimed in-service event, injury, or disease, regardless of whether such records mention the veteran by name, as long as the other requirements of paragraph (c) of this section are met;**
>
> **(ii)** Additional service records forwarded by the Department of Defense or the service department to VA any time after VA's original request for service records; and
>
> **(iii)** Declassified records that could not have been obtained because the records were classified when VA decided the claim.
>
> **(2)** Paragraph (c)(1) of this section does not apply to records that VA could not have obtained when it decided the claim because the records did not exist when VA

decided the claim, or because the claimant failed to provide sufficient information for VA to identify and obtain the records from the respective service department, the Joint Services Records Research Center, or from any other official source.

**(3) An award made based all or in part on the records identified by paragraph (c)(1) of this section is effective on the date entitlement arose** or the date VA received the previously decided claim, whichever is later, or such other date as may be authorized by the provisions of this part applicable to the previously decided claim.

**(4)** A retroactive evaluation of disability resulting from disease or injury subsequently service connected on the basis of the new evidence from the service department must be supported adequately by medical evidence. Where such records clearly support the assignment of a specific rating over a part or the entire period of time involved, a retroactive evaluation will be assigned accordingly, except as it may be affected by the filing date of the original claim

VA will do everything in their power to make it seem (if you win) that the new records have nothing to do with *why* you won. Be careful. You should cite §3.156(c) when you refile and make it very clear what you are asking for. Do not let them give you the bum's rush.

We have spoken of the Fenderson, or staged rating in a prior chapter. VA will try to say you get 0 percent from the 1990 filing date because they have no C&P exam on you from that time. I have looked at numerous claims, and they all have this in common. You win and kerwham—0 percent right up until the day you refiled this and then 100 percent. If you filed in 1990, you had symptoms, and it will be in your private records. These can be used to confirm the degree of your illness or injury all the way to the present. VA will fight hard for a while until you get all you're asking for. I doubt they will give it up without a fight. I have seen this take several years. VA often waits until five minutes before the BVA or CAVC decision and then throws in half the towel. You want the whole bath towel, the hand towel, and the matching washcloth. Do not settle for less.

# CHAPTER 8

# 38 CFR §3.156(b)

**Submitting New and Material Evidence during the Appeal**

This is a rare mistake, but VA has done it often in the past. Imagine a denial followed by a NOD. Okay, you happen to file new and material evidence with your NOD to prove something they said is wrong. Read this:

> **Pending claim.** New and material evidence received prior to the expiration of the appeal period, or prior to the appellate decision if a timely appeal has been filed (including evidence received prior to an appellate decision and referred to the agency of original jurisdiction by the Board of Veterans Appeals without consideration in that decision in accordance with the provisions of § 20.1304(b)(1) of this chapter), will be considered as having been filed in connection with the claim which was pending at the beginning of the appeal period.

VA may send you back a SOC that says, "Roger on the N&M evidence. We'll review this and get a new decision out to you pronto." You wait and wait. Nothing happens, and you think they just blew you off. You move on in life, and one day, you get sick or you discover you can't move without a wheelchair.

You file for a reopening of the old claim, and when you're doing this, you get your C-file. There's the new evidence you sent in and no denial. More importantly, there is no SOC saying, "Okay, dude, here's the SOC (or SSOC), and you have sixty days to file the Form 9." In other words, your old claim is still open because they took no action on it. This happened a *lot* in the early nineties, and the only way you will know is by examining your C-file. If you have filed in the past—for anything—I strongly suggest getting a copy of this before you refile. It will show you what they used to deny you in the past and reveal any negative or wrong information that may have been entered. I've had Vets who find other guy's paperwork from a different C-file mixed in with theirs. Paper systems are imperfect, and there is a lot of room for errors. VA's errors with paper files are what Murphy's Laws are all about.

When you win this version, they will use the same Fenderson staged rating system on it. Again, be prepared for a 0 percent rating and make plans to argue it with pertinent private records from your doctors. VA is very predictable when you win an old claim. They rush to block a meaningful settlement until you prove they are in error. It usually will take a year or more and a possible appeal if they want to be difficult. Relax. The only problem with any settlement is that they don't pay interest. Dollars awarded in 1990 are based on the compensation tables in effect in 1990. This is grossly unfair, but it's what we have to live with.

# CHAPTER 9

## VR&E FILINGS FOR THE INDEPENDENT LIVING PROGRAM

VA has many unique programs for Veterans with extensive disabilities. Some of us have numerous illnesses and injuries that render us unable to get out and do things. We are housebound because of this. To deal with it, VA offers the Independent Living Program (ILP). They used to be very generous, but with the government now poor, they are giving us less. Many Vets used to be able to finagle a computer out of them. In the past, a John Deere tractor was not out of the question. Getting anything nowadays is far more difficult. VA thinks installing grab bars next to the toilet will improve your quality of life. Watching Drew Carey on the *Price Is Right* is not mental entertainment for all Vets. Many can and have proven they can use computers to help the community or other Veterans. I am one. I am still fighting for one, but they did come out and look at the computer I am borrowing and measure me for a new one. It's on appeal. That's all I can say. And I get to add here in the final edit that they just approved me for one with all the bells and whistles as of April 2012. The reason? I filed a NOD and said I'd fight to the CAVC for it.

To access this program for benefits, you will need to contact the VA's Vocational Rehabilitation and Education office nearest you and ask to submit a claim for ILP benefits. This will begin a dog and pony show that even the Ringling Brothers Circus could be proud of. VA will run you through the video and a personalized interview to determine you are—yep—100 percent disabled. They will discover that—yep—you are not a candidate for retraining and thus entitled to ILP. After a month, they will send out a fellow who will check the bathrooms for grab bars and measure the hallways even if you aren't in a wheelchair. He/she will sit down with you and ask what you need. This is all for show. They have to be able to say they went through the motions before they deny you. This is true in everything VA does. I think it's called plausible denial. The appearance of justice for Veterans must always be observed. While this may seem to be a normal claims process, it isn't. This is handled by a fellow who has a degree in psychology or psychiatry. They are wise beyond their years and a legend in their own mind. They know better than you what you need to make your life more "independent." This will be the key word used in the denial so keep an eye out for it. Independence to you and me is much different from VA. Unless you can convince these guys you need something to stimulate your brain and help others, you won't get anywhere. Proof of an inability to drive or interact with your "community" will be evidence in your favor. A word to the wise. If you are asking for a computer and say you are using a borrowed one, don't be surprised if the investigator asks to look at it. They'll be searching for evidence of pornography downloads. They are not stupid. You need to prove things to win, just as you would with a claim for compensation. I have the asknod.org website, so my need is fairly evident. I suggest you start a Vet's blog now if you want to win one too. However, the final reason they granted mine was that I threatened to go to DC. I am convinced of that. Look on my website for this one:

http://asknod.wordpress.com/2012/05/03/independent-living-program-results/

VA also has a separate program to upgrade your home to make it

ADA-compliant if you are confined to a wheelchair. This is much easier to accomplish. They may even adapt a van for your transportation needs. You can find this out by contacting VA or a VSO. This type of assistance is much easier to win. VA rarely argues when you are service connected as long as your disabilities are clearly documented.

# CHAPTER 10

## EXAMPLE OF AN INITIAL CLAIM USING HCV AS AN EXAMPLE

You have two choices these days. You can file everything on VONAPP, which stands for Veterans Online Application, or you can go the traditional route. If you go the traditional route, there are the two paths we discussed in chapter 2. The choice between a VSO as "front man" or going pro se is the same. The choice of going VSO and letting them do it all means you don't have to buy this book. Of course, your chances of winning will go down to 12–15 percent too.

I like to have a nice paper file of everything I do for one reason. VA has a storied history of losing things. Computers crash and backup systems don't. A nice file in a cream-colored folder with all the things you are assembling is something you can grab as you leave when the house catches fire or the hurricane is upon you. You are going to put a lot of effort into this, and when VA says they never got something, you do not want to be there scratching your head and wondering what to do next. Depending on a VSO to be your mailman has been proved to be notoriously unreliable. They make mistakes. We all do, but this book will teach you all about calendars and how to read them.

You may choose to use VA's preprinted stuff like the Form 21-526 when you start or you can simply copy what they ask for onto my favorite Form 8.5 x 11. The VA is not your friend. I don't know how many Vets who have dutifully filled out everything VA asked for, including all five of their former wives details. They even assembled all the SSNs for the ex-wives and the SSNs of the offspring all for nothing. VA came back after they won and sent them off on a wild goose chase to find divorce decrees and death certificates again. This often is not resolved for years depending on the state in which you lived with your ex. You will be required to find and supply a divorce decree that was filed with the county auditor for each one. You will need birth certificates for each and every child you fathered and their SSNs. Knowing this ahead of time gives you something else to do on your long list while you wait. Do it, file it, and wait. If it's there when the win comes in, you'll get your funds sooner. They may ask for it again. Keep it handy in the "dependents" folder.

Assuming you chose to print up your own "forms," I suggest you use the format below. Assume the header is the top of your page. Each page must have your SSN and the page number on it in case they drop it and reassemble the pages in the wrong order (or file).

Page 1 123-45-6789

Dept. of Vet. Affairs
444 W. Fort Street
Boise, ID 83702-4531

April 1, 2012

Re: John Q. Sixpack
SSN 123-45-6789
Initial Claim

VETERANS ADMINISTRATION CLAIMS

## Initial Claim for Entitlement to Benefits

Dear Sir,

Enclosed please find my application for benefits for compensation. I wish to file for the following:

> Entitlement to Residuals of a liver disorder or hepatitis, not otherwise specified.

In addition I enclose the following: VA Form 21-526 (or a reasonable facsimile), which supplies all the information needed to process the claim, contemporary service treatment records (STRs) from service (exhibit A), postservice medical records documenting a current, chronic disease process (exhibit B) and a nexus letter from my doctor attesting that this was incurred during my service (exhibit C). In addition, I have a buddy letter(s) (exhibits D, E) from fellow Veteran(s) Billy Bob Sixkiller and Ralph S. Malph. They served with me in the _____ Infantry, ___ Company in I Corps while I was in Vietnam. Copies of their DD 214s are included in the evidence under exhibits F and G. I also include a statement from my wife attesting to my current health (exhibit H) and statements from my adult children that describe my gradually increasing debility (exhibits I and J). I have included internet articles that support my theory of transmission of hepatitis by poor hygiene before the advent of modern sterile procedures (exhibit K, L, M, N, and O). These articles are for the benefit of the rater and are not specific to me. However, the information contained in them is contemporaneous and demonstrates that the risk(s) were present during the time of my service.

While I am not a doctor and have no medical training, I believe that I contracted this: **(choose appropriate one)**

1. When I handled wounded soldiers or via wound received in combat in 2/3/1968 (blood exposure).
2. From multiuse pneumatic air injection devices used to administer inoculations during basic training.
3. From prostitutes where I contracted a sexually transmitted disease while in service.
4. From the unsterile needles used on my tattoo in _____ while in service.
5. From using shared razors and toothbrushes in service.
6. From _____ in service.
7. Transfusion following thru and thru gunshot wound to right leg on 2/3/1968.

Here, I would summarize the seminal event (or events) that you think are the cause and the approximate time (date) and circumstances if you know them.

Discuss probative articles that describe or support your contentions about your disease risks. Explain what the history of discovery was and the gradual increase in the disease process and its symptoms. Explain how this has impacted your life and your ability to work.

Explain that hepatitis A and B were not diagnosable until the Australian antigens test was developed in 1971. Explain that is was impossible to diagnose or identify hepatitis C until 1992 when the first Elysium RNA tests were available commercially; therefore, the VA examiner will find no mention of it in contemporary STRs prior to 1992.

Include buddy statements, affidavits from wife and children. Go to my Web site and download the articles on HCV that WGH posted in his claim.

Anything you submit to VA on your own stationery must include this exact phrase at the end:

> "The above statement is true and correct to the best of my knowledge and belief."

You must then sign it over your printed signature. VA Form 21-4138 has it incorporated into their signature block so signing it implies you read it and are so swearing. Make sure you put your SSN and the page number on *every page*, so they can find it after it falls on the floor with all the other Veterans' claims.

Signed
John Q. Sixpack
1234 Yellow Brick Road NW
Oz, Idaho 60609
Cel. 360-555-1212

Follow-on correspondence should include the same info in the header. When VA mails you something back such as a request for more info or a risk factors questionnaire, they will include a note in the upper right that says, "In reply, refer to: 357/RPG." It will always be a three-number/three-letter combination that will identify you and the motion or request you are responding to. Make sure you use this as they are pretty dense. This will help them screw up your claim instead of someone else's.

When you get your first denial, it will consist of the usual phrases of "Thank you for your service to America" and things like "We tried like the devil to make this puppy fly, but we find ourselves unable to grant the claim." Somewhere after the denial, there will be a summary of the evidence reviewed. Make sure they didn't "lose" the nexus letter that this whole thing hangs on. Make sure they didn't change the claim to residuals of a hemorrhoid when they mixed your claim up with another Vet's. In short, make sure they are giving your denial to you and not someone else's. It happens.

The denial will state the actual way they think your claim should have been worded. They almost always have to tamper with it for some reason. When they get done with it, it may say "entitlement to residuals of HCV." Below the denial, there will be a statement of **Reasons and Bases**. This will be a rambling, disjointed, and misspelled paragraph that tells you why they cannot grant it. There will be a long section semisummarizing the evidence against your claim. They may describe your evidence, but they will explain why theirs is better. If you provide a nexus letter that says it was jet guns, I can virtually guarantee a denial. The Gomers at the RO do not have permission to do this. It will have to go to DC. If you were in combat, you are accorded more deference, and they'll believe your story up to a point, unless you go down the jet gun road. Exposure to blood is assumed in combat everywhere but the VA. They think the risk should be recorded in your STRs along with every paper cut you ever had. For a while, Vets got denied because there was no record of them sharing razors or toothbrushes in the medrecs. Helloooo? Why would there be? The CAVC threw that one out in 2009. With all that said, I just had a Vet win a jet gun claim (of sorts) at the RO. It was a win based on blood exposure and jet guns. The VA examiner said the risks were in equipoise, and the Vet got the benefit of the doubt. He had four nexus letters. VA's nexus doctor simply agreed with no argument.

Most of you will immediately file a Notice of Disagreement (NOD) and start the process of moving it to DC. You can file a long letter disagreeing and include new evidence. It will be followed in about ten months with a Statement of the Case (SOC). VA will copy the denial and reprint it. This time, they will quote all the passages from 38 CFR they can assemble that deal with the reasons for the denial. If you submitted new evidence, they will have to send you a new denial and an SOC. An SOC cannot be used to announce a decision. It's against the law. A denial has to come in its own envelope. To cover your ass, you can then refile your NOD and start the whole process over again.

A denial following an SOC, where you contest it with new evidence, will result in a Supplemental Statement of the Case (SSOC). This will once again tell you why you're going to DC. The reason being, of course, is that they didn't cave in at the RO level. Many times your evidence is impeccable and bulletproof. VA will not let these little people adjudicate hepatitis B and C claims arising from "questionable" risks. They may send out for an IMO or an IME if you present enough Internet stuff to support it. A good nexus almost always will provoke an IMO/IME on a jet gun-based claim at the RO level. You can almost bet on it if the BVA remands back to the RO for an error. Always remember an Independent Medical Examination (IME) takes place without you being present. It just sounds like a C&P. Remember also in VA land that a gynecologist can do an orthopedic C&P. You, on the other hand, had best have a licensed and approved orthopedic surgeon.

## Back Injury

My second example here will be a claim based on a back injury. Your claim should follow the same protocols as the hepatitis claim above except for the claim wording. This one will say:

**Entitlement to compensation for back injury, not otherwise specified.**

Remember, no doctors allowed. Just back injury. No DDD, sciatica, radiculopathy, or scoliosis. You may have all the evidence in the world, but you cannot call it DDD. You can say where it hurts, when it hurts, and how painful it is—period. If it's in your STRs (also called SMRs), then you can point to this as the day it occurred. A noting of this in the medical records is the gold standard for the claim. If VA doesn't have a bunch of evidence that says it healed up in service and you were good to go, then it is assumed to be chronic. Chronic means continuing on for years and years to the present. Acute means an injury that has healed and is no longer a problem. If they called it acute in service, you must prove that the symptoms were chronic and continued to this day. You must have the medical records to prove it too. If you file a claim thirty years after service and start seeing the doctor a month before your claim, it won't work. If this is truly related to service and chronic, it would bother you day in and day out from the day you separated. Your claim has to have legs (continuity). Without it, you are doomed.

Some of you may be filing injuries related to shrapnel (shell fragment wound or SFW) or gunshot wounds (GSWs). Sometimes these injuries will flare up when you get older. Cold weather is often a culprit. You will need the proof it was incurred in service to win. A Purple Heart is all you need. These injuries do not have to surface within a set number of years like a back claim. If your medical records are lost, the medal is proof you were wounded in combat.

Some injuries are just because of old age or obesity. You can try to hang them on VA, but they rarely grant unless the evidence is overwhelmingly in your favor. If you have DM2 and are overweight, even though this is a presumptive from herbicides used in Vietnam, expect a fight. It may go to the BVA for a win, and it shouldn't have to. If you had it or symptoms of it before you got to Vietnam, you'll lose.

## PTSD Claims

Phrase this one carefully. You have no medical training, so you cannot prediagnose yourself. My suggestion would be to use something like:

> Entitlement to service connection for major mental disorder not otherwise specified.

## VETERANS ADMINISTRATION CLAIMS

These used to be as hard as, or harder, than hepatitis claims. Any mental illness is similar for filing purposes. You have to have a diagnosis of bent brain from a shrink as you probably know. Now (as of 2010) you have to get it from a VA-approved one. You need to have a pertinent stressor (sexual assault—male *or* female, combat, etc.) that made you fear for your life. It has to have had a marked impact on your work history, your social interaction with others, and certain exhibited effects that can be documented by the brain doctor. This is called a stressor. The medical measurement of this is called your GAF score. GAF stands for "global assessment of functioning." The lower the GAF score, the more bent you are. When you get down to forty-five, you're usually not married anymore or working. Many Vets often have a raging drug habit from this. SSI may have given you a pension by now too. This is considered important proof by VA.

PTSD was not diagnosed under this name before 1982. I'm sure it has a long history of names such as "shellshock," "combat fatigue," and "mental disorder NOS" (not otherwise specified). The military was fond of giving us the boot when we came home from Vietnam with "stress" symptoms. These were called personality disorders rather than mental illness. The difference is simple. VA pays for diagnosed mental disorder. They do not pay for antisocial personality with passive-aggressive tendencies. You can guess what the Army and Air Force shrinks were instructed to write down. Many Vets didn't get any help for years and even decades until this barrier was broken down. Some still haven't won and have given up. I'm sure you know some, like me. My illness has resolved over forty years, but the sound of a Huey flying over ruins my day with old memories. To add insult, a lot of pilots train their students over my rural area as it's near an airport. Small single-engine four-bangers like the O-1 I flew in sound similar, so that is another irritant. An iPod solves most of it. I'm lucky. My second wife understands me and the problem.

Where combat is concerned as a stressor, there must be evidence of this. VA has recently changed the rules, but they are still stringent. You will now have to convince a VA doctor that you have compensable issues. You probably won't have evidence of this in your service treatment records (STRs). Most guys didn't come unglued until they got their nose out of the drugs or the alcohol wore off.

Convincing VA to grant any claim hinges on how strong your claim is, how well prepared you are, and whether it's easier to grant than it is to fight. Since 85 percent lose and give up, it's important to look smart and have a claim that looks professional. Where PTSD is concerned, I strongly suggest a VSO or a good friend who is a Vet from your era. Going at it alone with this disease has a really poor win ratio. You need all your wits about you *all* the time. I don't think it's fair to you to say you'll win if you follow this recipe. PTSD is a mental illness just as serious as schizophrenia or bipolar disorders. Don't waste your time on this book. You could ask a VSO to buy it and play by these rules, though I doubt they will.

Your chances of winning are directly proportional to how aggressive you are. Don't confuse this with anger of rudeness. Sending in letters that say you think VA employees are brain-dead because of what they did to your claim won't help. They mean well, but they are brainwashed. They are trained to deny. They can't and won't admit this. In their mind, they are tasked with looking at a lot of evidence. If it doesn't fit neatly into the equation, it is discarded or put in the reject pile. No evidence is automatically negative evidence. It's purely deductive thinking with no room for variables. To the VA, all Vets are the same and want something—money. VA's job is to decide who is worthy and who isn't. This is why some who don't deserve to win do and vice versa.

VA says they do a benefit of the doubt (BOTD) dance at the end of every claim. If the evidence "for" is more than the evidence "against", you win. If it's equal, you're supposed to win. Most decisions that VA says are granted based on benefit of the doubt are ones where the evidence was totally in the Vet's favor. For this reason, I believe the game is rigged against the Vet. Nothing can change my mind. The only way to win at this is to make everything submitted say one thing—grant my claim. Speculative or equivocal arguments from articles or studies will be used against you. Make everything you present say one thing and one thing only—here's my proof. No "could be," "might have," "it's possible that," "within the realm of possibility," etc., may be used.

Scientific proof of something only allows for one conclusion to the exclusion of all others. Even though Occam's razor argues that the simplest reason is almost always the cause, you do not want to rely on it. VA will find a way to turn it against you. A nexus does this in no uncertain terms. Even though it is speculative, it's *informed and reasoned* speculation by a professional schooled in it. That's what this will boil down to in the end. I worry for Vets with this new rule change. If VA gets to use their doctors, what then? It doesn't seem fair to have the judge *and* the jury chosen from your enemies. If you do have a private nexus from your treating physician I would submit it. It sure can't hurt. VA will have to at least look at it.

## Postgame Wrap

I make no promises that every one of you, or any of you will win. I will say that you *should* win based on the theory. I have helped twenty-nine Vets win or get an increase. Some were very difficult, and some were easy. Everyone did it themselves with my occasional advice. I didn't do it personally. Virtually, all of them are 100 percent P&T. Several had to go to DC. Most didn't. We have two who will never win because of lost records. We have two whose willful misconduct or character of discharge prevented them even if it was service connected. And then we have one where the Vet wanted me to do it all and got mad at me when he was denied. I tried to help do the appeal, but everything I did wasn't up to par or wasn't timely enough. I gave up in order to save my health. That much negative energy is harmful. Please do not be disappointed if you lose at the RO. It is a stepping stone to eventual victory. This whole process is unique to each one of you. There is no "standard" claim. I accept no liability for what you do or do not accomplish with this book. It represents all I have observed for twenty-three years about the process. VA is not your friend. That is what I know now. Good luck, and thank you for your unselfish contribution to America's continued freedom. Without you, English might not be our first language.

## DBQs
## Disability Benefits Questionnaires

As a postscript to this, VA has just come out with what they call DBQs, or disability benefits questionnaires. They would dearly love to have you or your private physician fill them out. Be very careful. These forms have no provisions for a nexus letter from your doctor. If you submit one, VA will invariably provide their own, and I think you know by now that the nexus they provide will be negative and unsupportive. VA also says these forms will speed up your claim. We have been hearing how they are going to speed things up since I first filed in 1989. I have yet to see anything showing improvement in twenty-odd years. According to all the articles on this, the backlog continues to increase, and the time needed to resolve an initial claim has increased from six months to over two years or more. Some of the easy ones, like dependency issues, are done in ten months.

Here's the link for the DBQs:
http://benefits.va.gov/TRANSFORMATION/dbqs/ListByDBQFormName.asp

And by symptom or disease:

http://benefits.va.gov/TRANSFORMATION/dbqs/ListBySymptom.asp

    I hope this helps all of you, even though I know some will be left behind. I have tried to look for anything that can be of use. My Website at asknod.org is always available and has been for four years. One of my assistants or I will gladly answer your questions. The e-mail address is asknod@gmail.com. Always remember this is dynamic law that is changing—usually in the Vets' favor.

    On matters of law, I have not discussed much to avoid lawsuits. I am not a lawyer and have no training in it. I offer observations and personal experiences. If you lose, please do not blame me for it. Everything I have assembled here is simply based on what I have done and the outcomes of others I have helped. Always remember that this process is unique to each one of you. The general claims outline is similar for all types. Claims for an increase are no different but sometimes require a note from your doctor. Bon chance!

AskNod
2012

```
      \\!//
      (o o)
 -oOOo-(_)-oOOo-
```

CPSIA information can be obtained
at www.ICGtesting.com
Printed in the USA
BVHW03s2205140618
519154BV00001B/11/P